NORSE PAGANISM GUIDE

Religions Of the Norse, Norse Shamanism, Norse Deities, Nine Realms, Monsters in Norse and Many more!

ALTHENEA CROWLEY

PREFACE

The hallowed domain of Norse Shamanism is where the pulse of the earth and age-old murmurs merge in a mystical dance. As we journey through the world of Midgard in search of knowledge, healing, and the magic contained in the age-old customs and tales, may the spirits of the North lead and inspire us.

ACKNOWLEDGEMENT

Sincere gratitude flows to the ancestors and sages who illuminated the path of Norse Shamanism in the twilight of the Norse realms.

Contents

- **CHAPTER ONE** 5
- A HISTORY OF NORSE PAGANISM 5
- **CHAPTER TWO** 13
- MYTHS AND LEGENDS 13
- **CHAPTER THREE** 23
- RELIGIONS OF THE NORSE 23
- **CHAPTER FOUR** 36
- NORSE SHAMANISM 36
- **CHAPTER FIVE** 47
- NORSE DEITIES AND GODS 47
- **CHAPTER SIX** 62
- THE UNDERWORLD'S ALMIGHTY – HELL 62
- **CHAPTER SEVEN** 70
- NINE REALMS 70
- **CHAPTER EIGHT** 76
- MONSTERS IN NORSE MYTHOLOGY 76
- **CHAPTER NINE** 88
- THE PRESENCE OF KINGS AND PRIESTS IN NORSE PAGANISM
  88
- **CHAPTER TEN** 94
- ANCIENT SYMBOLS AND DEPICTIONS 94
- **CHAPTER ELEVEN** 122
- NORSE MAGIC 122
- **CHAPTER TWELVE** 131
- MYSTICISM AND ANIMISM IN NORSE MYTHOLOGY 131

CHAPTER ONE

A HISTORY OF NORSE PAGANISM

The term "Norse Paganism" describes a pre-Christian Scandinavian religion that dates back to the Iron Age Germanic people. The Norse Pagan religion persisted until Scandinavia was converted to Christianity. Due to military and commercial interests, the movement saw and welcomed the widespread conversion of many kings at the start of this era. There was a period when there was perfect harmony between the two religions, despite the fact that many kings became Norse pagans and some common people became Christians.

Many religious groups converted to the Old Norse Religion as a result of the modern era's surge in popularity of Norse paganism. In certain nations, Asatru, an Old Norse religion, is acknowledged as an official religion. Norse Paganism is a religion in which followers embrace traditional spiritual practices and beliefs that can be traced back to the Norse people of old. It is simple to link Norse to the

"Vikings," but this was only one type of Norse occupation, and not all of the people who lived there were Vikings. Like other people, the Norse had a variety of professions and lifestyle choices. Additionally, their opinions and values diverged. Among themselves, the Norse people practiced and shared cultural beliefs.

The Age of Vikings

The Middle Ages period known as the Viking Age (793–1066 CE) was primarily a time of Norse paganism. During this time, Norsemen or Northmen, also known as Vikings, engaged in widespread raids, as well as colonization, conquest, and trade activities across Europe and Northern America. The Germanic Iron Age and the migration era were succeeded by this one. The Scandinavian homeland and any place or places the Scandinavians settled are considered to be part of the Viking age. European history was negatively impacted by the Norsemen's raids and colonization of various European regions between the ninth and the eleventh centuries. The men from modern-day Sweden, Norway, and Denmark made up the pagans' warriors.

Their actions were caused by a few things. First of all, the Vikings were a group of notable individuals that included chieftains and clan leaders who possessed land and aimed to conquer and seize additional territory while enslaving people. Freemen and young men inspired by better opportunities outside their boundaries also made up the Viking population. Plus, there was the need to spread affluent towns and wealthy monasteries throughout these fragile kingdoms. The Vikings' exodus from their native lands may also have been influenced by overpopulation, poor farming, and political unrest emanating from the unified Norway. The aggressive expansion of the Carolingian Empire and the forced conversion of nearby Saxons to Christianity might have been the last contributing factor.

A few locations developed into the Norse people's (also known as Varangians') principal cities. Ireland, Iceland, Faroe Island, and other locations are among them. Additionally, these people made their first brief settlement in North America in Newfoundland. The Vikings were independent farmers when they were at home, but when they were at sea, they raided and pillaged. During the Viking era, the Norse homelands expanded by uniting into larger kingdoms.

England

The Lindisfarne Abbey was destroyed by the Vikings during their invasion of England in 793. This was considered to be the beginning of the Viking Age. Some contend and think that the Viking era could be brought back to the years 700–750. It was thought that it was unlikely that the attack on Lindisfarne in England was the first. Archaeological evidence suggests that Scandinavians were in contact with the British Isles early in the century. The Vikings did not conduct many raids in the earlier centuries, but this changed significantly in the ninth century. The monks in the abbey perished in the Lindisfarne attack. Together with the theft of the church's valuables, some of them were also thrown into the sea to drown, and others were taken prisoner and sold into slavery.

Alfred the Great's Wessex could not be subdued, even with the attacks in England. They therefore agreed to a ceasefire with him in 878, which served as the impetus for a treaty shortly after 886. From 892 to

The new Viking armies put up a strong fight in 899, but Alfred defeated them. The English raid, which was initiated by the Vikings in 980, eventually brought the nation under the control of the Canute Empire. That being said, in 1042 the native house was peacefully restored, putting an end to the Vikings' threats and attacks.

Ireland, Vinland, and the Western Seas

Scandinavian immigration to England was not limited to that nation. Additionally, they grew into other European nations. The expansion reached almost every location and extended to the western seas. About 900 people arrived in Iceland, and Greenland attempted to found colonies in North America after receiving settlers from Iceland. In the same time frame, there was an increase in the number of settlers in areas like Orkney,

Faroe, and The Shetlands, which included the Isle of Man and the Hebrides.

The archeological discoveries at L'Anse aux Meadows, on the northern tip of Newfoundland Island, demonstrated that the Viking transition was linked to regions where wild grapes were found, at least as far south as they went. Records date back to 795, when the unidentified island of Rechru was devastated by a Scandinavian invasion. The rise of the Scandinavians was once also observed in Waterford, Limerick, and Dublin. The kings of Dublin had strong feelings about the foreign adventurers at that time. Several Scandinavians ruled Northumberland and Dublin at the beginning of the tenth century. With the help of Orkney and some Irish villagers, the Irish Scandinavians were soundly defeated in the Clontarf Battle in 1014. There existed a possibility that Ireland would unite under Scandinavian domination. Even in the twelfth century, the English invaders found that the Scandinavians, despite being Christianized, still dominated major Irish cities like Cork, Limerick, Dublin, and Waterford, despite their severe defeat.

The Empire of France and the Carolingians

It was challenging for the Vikings to prevail and establish themselves on the British island because of the formidable defenses of the Carolingian Empire. Outside of Normandy, the

Scandinavians have had very little influence on the institutions and languages of the European continent. Up to the end of the Viking Age, there was a great deal of irregular raiding. A mixture of Normandy and Dutch Vikings lived in the Seine River settlement in the tenth century. But during Charlemagne's empire, the Vikings accomplished nothing more. The Viking raid reached the coasts of the Mediterranean and the Iberian Peninsula, extending much further south than France. There were fewer settlements because, despite their best efforts, they were unable to accomplish their goal as they had in other locations.

Europe's East

The Vikings' migration into Eastern Europe was not as violent as their expansion along the Atlantic coast. There were numerous irregular raids in the Baltic. Even though some Viking kingdoms were established in this region, none of them came to be through bloodshed. During the Viking era, the eastern movement was very successful and helped the Vikings reach the center of Russia. They ruled over cities like Novgorod and Kyiv despite having a very hard time getting inside the region. The Slavonic people were able to quickly assimilate them despite their dominance in these areas, which is how they came to be known as Rus, or "Russians."

There seemed to be a new Viking movement toward the east in the first part of the eleventh century. Swedish runic stones of men who accompanied Yngvarr on his journey have been documented. Additionally, the Scandinavians expanded their operations eastward and employed soldiers in Constantinople, Istanbul. As a result, the Byzantine Emperor's Varangian Guard was established. The chief of the Viking era vanished in the eleventh century, having served no useful purpose.

Neither Sweden nor Norway had an outside force that was more daring.

The greatest period of Norse paganism was practiced during the Viking Age. The Vikings brought their religious customs with them when they invaded and conquered every region of Europe and South America, which resulted in the spread of religion. The Christian Scandinavian era began with the end of the Viking Age. According to a number of historical accounts, the 11th century marked the end of the Viking Age and the significant decline of Norse paganism.

The 1800s

In the historical context of Norse paganism, various degrees of cross-cultural dissemination occurred among nearby populations, such as the Sami and Finns. After a protracted period of time, Norse paganism came to an end in the 11th century and was replaced by Christianity. The sole manifestations of Norse Paganism were found in Scandinavian folklore. Members of the Romanticist movement developed a renewed interest in Norse paganism in the 19th century. The inspiration used in a number of artworks during this time period was one of the main effects of Norse paganism.

It drew political interest figures as well. As a result, a number of nationalist organizations began embracing the antiquated religious doctrine and customs. Academic study on the topic started in the 19th century, when the sentiment of the pervasive romanticists had an influence.

CHAPTER TWO
MYTHS AND LEGENDS

The popular term for the Germanic branch of religion that emerged during the Proto-Norse period is Norse Paganism, also known as the Old Norse Religion. At this point, the North Germanic people split off to become a distinct group within the Germanic peoples. It was replaced by Christianity during the Christianization of the Scandinavians, leading to its forgetfulness. During this time, Old Norse religion was polytheistic. It allows for the worship or belief in a variety of gods, meaning that a practicing person may have faith in several deities. In Norse mythology, these gods are divided into two groups: the Çsir and the Vanir. It is believed that the Çsir and Vanir engaged in conflict with each other before coming to terms with the fact that neither was superior to the other and uniting into a single pantheon. The most well-known gods and goddesses in Norse mythology are Odin and Thor.

In Norse mythology, giants, spirits, dwarfs, elves, and other mystical beings are all around us. The center of Norse mythology was Yggdrasil, a massive ash tree that connected the nine worlds and was sometimes referred to as the "world tree." Yggdrasil contained several independently existing realms. The human realm of Midgard was one of these realms. There was also a realm for the afterlife, or life after death. A particular deity oversaw or rather ruled each realm.

The main focus of Norse paganism is on sacrifices and rituals. For these rites or sacrificial activities, chiefs and kings had equal responsibility. To complete these ritual practices, several locations were needed. Originally, these activities were carried out in outdoor areas like groves and lakes. After the third century, when cult houses were built solely for the purpose of performing rituals, this began to change. Still, a lot of people used the outdoor areas for a very long period. A type of sorcery or shamanic practice known as Seiðr was also a part of the Old Norse religion. There were also a variety of funerals performed, including inhumations and cremations, along with various grave offerings.

The Conviction of Norse Mythology

The diversity of beliefs was one aspect of Norse paganism that was shared by all. It depicted lessons about how the world we live in is shared by humans, various gods, and mystical creatures. The religion has a number of well-known gods, such as Odin, Thor, and Freya.

Beyond Norse paganism, these gods and the belief in their strength permeated English tradition. Norse paganism prescribed certain days for the worship of these deities. These beliefs are still reflected in the names we give to the days of the week. As an illustration, we observe:

Woden's Day: Wednesday is the day of the week that Odin, also known as Woden, brought us.

Thor's Day: Thursday, the fifth day of the week, was given its name in remembrance of the Viking god Thor.

Freya's Day: It is observed on Fridays, the sixth day of the week, as a way to honor the goddess.

The old Norse religion contained a variety of beliefs. These beliefs encompassed doctrines pertaining to cosmology, the afterlife, and other entities. Regretfully, a large portion of the Norse religion's original doctrines and guidelines were transmitted orally. The literature from the ancient times, when Norse Paganism was prevalent, is extremely sparse. Folklore and children's stories serve as the basis for a large portion of the religion's current doctrine and narratives. Others date back to the 19th century, when academics and educators began studying the faith. This implies that there will definitely be multiple interpretations and teachings on different facets and tenets of the religion's adherents. Certain teachings are thought to be more genuine and applicable to earlier periods than others. We'll look at more genuine teachings and what they have to say about the religious beliefs of the Norse.

The Afterlife

Different theories regarding death and the afterlife were developed in relation to Norse paganism.

Although ideology claims that people's post-death destinations were determined by moral considerations, Norse paganism rejected this theory. Rather, the warriors' souls that were about to die were transferred to Odin's great hall, Valhalla, where they rested until Ragnarok, when they would rise once more to battle the Çsir.

540 doors were provided by Valhalla to those whose souls rested there. Grimnismál, a poem, tells of an eagle soaring overhead and a wolf guarding the western door. The poem also tells of Heiðrún, a goat that gave an endless supply of mead, and Saehrimnir, a boar that was killed and eaten every day but rose again the next morning. What is unknown is how the Norsemen's society perceived Valhalla. Some speculate that it might have been nothing more than a literary creation meant to appease the aspirations and hopes of the ruling class. Its foundation was the notion that the social structure of warriors and their lord was equal to that of dead warriors serving Odin in the military.

Beyond the warriors of ancient Scandinavia, there were others who believed in an afterlife. Elderly people or those who passed away from illness or disease would travel to a place called Fólkvangr, which is another word for Hell. The afterlife was never mentioned as being in Hell in any of the pagan skaldic poetry. Usually, "Hell" is referred to as the goddess of the same name. Dead Viking warriors were probably sent to Sindri, in the Niðafjöll Mountains, or to Gimlé, to the Hall of Brimir. Various sagas, such as the Eddaic poem Helgakviða Hjörvarðssonar, depicted the dead as still existing in their graves and claiming to be conscious. These works from the 13th century suggest that ghosts, or Draugr, may still haunt the living.

Both the Laxdæla Saga and the Eyrbyggja Saga have connections between pagan burials and hauntings. Odin was the god most closely associated with death in some mythological stories. The Poetic Edda poem Hávamál discusses Odin's relationship with the dead. The poem's stanza 138 describes Odin's self-sacrifice by hanging himself from Yggdrasil, the world tree. He attempted to acquire mystical abilities and wisdom by doing this for nine nights.

In the end of the Gautreks saga, King Vikarr was also hanged. The king was pierced with a spear, and the executioner said, "Now I give you to Oðinn."

Demise

The Norse religion holds certain beliefs regarding death. The greatest thing a human can hope for is to die valiantly in combat. Warriors or Vikings who died valiantly in the face of battle were thought to have winged female spirits known as Valkyries descend to gather and transfer their souls to be with Odin at Valhalla, the place the Vikings considered to be heaven.

The warriors would feast at Odin's side after their souls had been transported to Valhalla, eating and drinking whatever they pleased as they willed eternity away. Still, the afterlife did not send the souls of fallen Vikings only to Valhalla. Another goddess who attracted a lot of Viking warrior souls was Freya. Even more than those in Valhalla, dead Viking warriors who managed to reach Freya's exquisite palace, known as Fólkvangr, would eat, drink, and revel in all of its lovely moments. There was a place for warriors who were unable to travel to either of Odin's or Freya's magnificent places of eternal abode for their fallen warriors. Hell, which is the third place the Vikings were prepared for, could be reached by a dead Viking warrior.

It was thought that passing away marked the beginning of a new journey rather than the actual end of a life. That's why, whether they spent their lives with Odin, Freya, or in hell, they went to great lengths to prepare their dead for the afterlife. Not only were they not buried alone, but they were interred alongside everything that held significance for them, such as gold, swords, axes, exquisite apparel, and other possessions they cherished during their lifetime. The idea was that they would require these things for their trip to the great beyond. Because of this, Viking burial sites are highly valued by modern historians and archaeologists because they may have evidence of priceless treasures and other artifacts that belonged to the Vikings.

Universe

Textual sources contained several narratives about the cosmogony of Norse paganism or the mythical creation myth. Nevertheless, there is no proof that these were created prior to Christianity. Possibilities exist that they developed at the same time as Christianity did, as pagans attempted to create a creation myth sufficiently intricate to rival Christianity. The setting and order of events are referred to as part of Norse paganism's cosmology. It was thought that this place was more of a spiritual environment or world than a physical one. Even though it was an invisible world, there were a few instances in which the Vikings' spiritual and material worlds coincided. While shamanic tradition cosmologies in northern Eurasia may have shared certain aspects with Norse pagan cosmologies, their interpretation of these shared patterns was presented as distinct from other perspectives. The trunk of Yggdrasil was discovered to be at the center of the universe. The roots of Yggdrasil contained nine distinct worlds, each of which served as the home of a different kind of non-physical entity that ruled the Norse otherworld, which included the human world. Nonetheless, the following is a provisional list of the nine worlds, sourced from this era, despite the lack of an explicit list of their homelands: -

It was thought that Midgard was the birthplace of both humanity and human civilization.

The world of the Aesir tribe of gods and goddesses was thought to be Asgard.

The world of the gods and goddesses of the Vanir tribe is called Vanaheim.

The world of Jotunheim was devoted to the Giants.

Niflheim was an ice-dominated primordial world.

Muspelheim, the world of primordial fire.

Alfheim was the home of the elves.

Svartalfheim, or Nidavellir, was the dwarfs' home planet.

Hel was the realm of the dead and the goddess of the same name.

Beings

In Norse mythology, the female deities were referred to by the Norns as being in charge of determining a person's fate. As far as Snorri knew, there were three categories for the Norns. But it was also acknowledged—not just by Snorri but by other sources as well—that the fate of a newborn was decided by the elder Norns. It is unclear, nevertheless, if these goddesses were revered by the populace. It was thought that the land spirits, known as vættir, resided in waterfalls, mountains, rocks, and trees, and that humans used to sacrifice and offer offerings to them. In certain spheres of everyday existence, it was also thought that Norns held greater significance than the gods. The texts also mentioned a few elves and dwarves. Relationships were found between specific individuals or families and some Flygjur, the guardian spirits. It was thought that these guardian spirits were typically female, as were other supernatural beings such as the dísir, Hamingjur, and swanmaidens who lacked a set stature. Among these female deities, Disir might have served as a tutelary goddess.

Odin and the Valkyries had a relationship regarding myths pertaining to the god of the Vikings. They were also depicted in heroic poetry, like Helgi Lays, where it was thought that they played the role of princesses assisting in the marriages of heroes. The battle with the giants, also known as J tnar, was another recurring theme in mythology. The mythology claimed that the j ɨ tnar were related to and the ancestors of the gods. The goddesses would not interact with the giants, even though the gods married giantesses. Some scholars claim that the j ɨ tnar were not worshipped, but this claim has drawn a lot of criticism. The j ɨ tnar of the Eddaic tradition were thought to be wiser than their folkloric counterparts, despite similarities between the two.

CHAPTER THREE
RELIGIONS OF THE NORSE

The various rituals that the Norse pagans practiced before the Christian religion emerged were part of their religious practices. Folk religion, as opposed to organized religion, was practiced by the Norse people. Nonetheless, the survival and social regeneration of Norse paganism served a single purpose. As a result, rather than having stronger ties to families and the village, the Norse faith became more dispersed. Numerous religious festivals have also been documented, and religious leaders have overseen the people's and society's faith.

A person had to be the head of a family before being considered worthy of leading the faith, and the faith leader was revered as the king across the country. Norse religion was centered around specific practices like sacred acts, god worship, and rituals. Before Christianity arrived, the Scandinavians had no word for religion, but they did have a word that was similar to it: "sidr," which means "custom." Paganism was called "forn sidr," which translates to "old or ancient custom." Norse paganism never stayed uniform in its practice; it never had the same composition or structure. But it was composed of a number of related traditions and beliefs, many of which had been passed down through the generations. Geographical distances occasionally played a role in the diversity of cultural experiences that the Scandinavians encountered. The mythologies and poetic traditions of the people were better understood by one another.

Nearly every ritual that people were familiar with or performed in the modern practice of this religion involved a Blót, which was a type of sacrifice in the Norse religion. The calendar feasts were also greatly influenced by the communal feasts, wherein sacrificial meat, mead, and occasionally bread were consumed. Grain and other food items were utilized as sacrifices in regular rituals. There was much more to these sacrifices than simply eating these meats or drinking mead. Their primary goal was to promote fertility and community growth. These acts of sacrifice were, nevertheless, also performed in connection with marriages, births, and funerals.

In the era of Norse paganism, there was a distinct division between private and public faith. The customs were associated with the person or a particular family. Alternatively, it had to do with the social order.

However, it is difficult to determine the exact degree to which the myths that are known were associated with the beliefs of the Scandinavian people prior to the arrival of Christianity. Furthermore, it is unclear how much of the people's behavior was directed toward different religious rituals in their day-to-day lives. The Scandinavians claim that all Christian texts are biased and misinterpreted, and they are unable to locate any sources regarding Norse religious practices. This occurred as a result of the Christian religion's perception of the Norse religion as superstitious, which was based mostly on how much devotion and homage they paid to the devil. Although Norse paganism appeared to be negatively viewed by Christianity, certain archeological evidence to the contrary has been discovered. Its interpretation is challenging to comprehend, though, and it is separate from written materials.

Customs

The religion of Norse paganism is predicated on a number of ritual activities. The Norse pagans thought that their gods were an integral part of their everyday existence. This was particularly true for soldiers who cared to involve their gods in nearly every action they took while fighting. Consequently, these believers appeased the gods by performing rituals and offering sacrifices. Large-scale religious rites were performed by Norse pagans at the homes of nobles as a way of paying homage to the gods. All the Norse Pagans ascribed their devotion to one of the many gods; the most devoted were to Odin, Thor, and Loki. Although each god had his own religious customs, most Norse god rites were performed in the same way.

Seid

One of the older Nordic religious rites was this one. Along with other religious practices, this has been demonstrated through documented evidence over time. Of all the Norse rituals, this one was by far the most bizarre. Seid was viewed as having elements of magic that went beyond traditional Norse customs and culture. This was among the first causes of the early Christians' disconnection from the religion of the Norsemen. Seid had strong ties to important mythological stories, which added a layer of religious complexity. Odin was said to have learned this from Freyja. Still, most people agree that Seid was considered the most important aspect of Norse paganism. It is quite challenging to ascertain from the sources what the term meant during the Viking era. On the other hand, Seid is most commonly associated with being a ritual used for omen interpretation and divination. Although these omens might have been favorable, they might also have been manipulated negatively.

Runes

Reputable academic sources have described runes as extremely potent symbols with strong ties to Odin, one of the gods of Norse paganism. Runes were employed in various ceremonies.

Ritual Locations

For many of the older traditions, there were no ritually designated locations. When the powers of nature accompanied them, the ancient shamans and religious leaders conducted religious ceremonies or rituals outdoors. This included all of the above, as well as areas around fire pits, mountains, and large bodies of water. Sacred sites and ritual houses were constructed over time, but their popularity did not last long. In due course, these built ritual sites were accepted by the populace and utilized for ritualistic activities. Norse pagans or those who are fervent about the religion continue to actively explore a number of ritual sites in contemporary practices.

One of the Norse Pagan ritual sites was in Iceland.

These ceremonial locations served as educational centers for Norse paganism, their gods, and goddesses, and were associated with pre-Christian Scandinavian traditions. People started congregating in Thingvellir about the year 930, with the representatives of each tribe holding yearly meetings there. This once-in-a-year gathering continued till 1798. An occurrence happened in 1944 when Icelanders gathered at the same location to celebrate the nation's freedom from Denmark. The site Thingvellir had geological and religious significance. It sat on the fault between the Eurasian and North American tectonic plates. Aside from that, it spiritually symbolized the heart of Iceland, and many people from Iceland believed that a visit to Thingvellir provided you with a feeling of being in a "powerful place." The Snæfellsnes glacier is located atop what is popularly known as the most attractive Iceland mountain.

In the history of Iceland, as written in the Sagas, they identified Snæfellsnes as an entrance to the underworld. Moreover, in the base of Snæfellsnes lay Mary's well. Located on the North Coast of the Snæfellsnes peninsula was Helgafell. In the ancient period, Helgafell was referred to as a place of pilgrimage. This special place was specifically dedicated to those about to die. Helgafell was believed to have been the opening or entrance into life after death. Most people believed that at the peak of Helgafell, you could easily take a look at Odin's kingdom, Valhalla, a paradise of warriors, especially those that had died while in battle.

Norse pagans, or those interested in or adhering to the religion, will stop at nothing to reach the summit of Helgafell in the modern world. They act in this way in the hopes of fulfilling their three wishes—especially if they follow the holy guidelines. One of the rules is to not look back and to concentrate only on the future. Second, climbers are required to remain silent until they have completed their wishes, without saying a word. And lastly, you must keep your wishes to yourself if you want to reach the summit of the mountain.

Offerings

Norse religion, or paganism, is characterized by numerous sacrifices, or "Blóts." Various texts claim that scarifications were a part of Norse paganism, and were used to help the people deal with a variety of problems and crises. It served as a way to express gratitude for favors given on other occasions. The sacrifices used were very similar to those made in other religions. The method of sacrifice, though, was very distinct from others. There had to be bloodshed for any sacrifice made in Norse paganism. This was primarily accomplished by slaughtering various animals in accordance with the sacrifice's intended use.

In Heimskringla, Hákon the Good states that some Blóts are required, and in this case, animals were killed and slaughtered. Temple altars were sprinkled with their blood, or hlaut as it was called, both inside and outside. During the sacrifice feasts, people would wine, eat, and dine while making the customary toast. As part of a custom, the chieftain would consecrate the food and pass the cups over the fire.

Adam of Bremen described the Uppsala and included information about a festival that takes place every nine years.

Numerous male animals were sacrificed for this festival, and their bodies were hung over the Temple's grove. Numerous sacrificial techniques have been discussed over time, but one aspect consistently surfaces in all of them: the head of the sacrificed animal was always hung on a tree or mounted on a pole. The animal blot happened before a duel, before traders made agreements with one another, before a merchant or sailor sailed, and occasionally at funerals. The aforementioned assertion is supported by the discovery of diverse animal remains in a variety of Old Norse burial sites during archeological excavations. According to the story of Ibn Fadlan's ship burial, dogs were frequently offered as sacrifices. Hens, cows, oxen and draft horses, roosters, and occasionally a serving girl were also discovered. Blóta means "worshiping with a sacrificial blood" or "to strengthen." Old Norse paganism, which involved animal sacrifices as a form of worship, was also prevalent, according to a number of sources, archeological evidence, and records. Horses and pigs were specifically among these animals. Each animal played a significant part in the blot activities. Blóta was a major sacrifice performed by Norse pagans in the Sacral structures; it was not a standard sacrifice, out of all the rituals. There was a necessity to kill animals in a blot, closer in concept to a gift. Human blood was occasionally needed as a sacrifice. The blood from the animals that were sacrificed was either sprinkled on top of the stones or collected in a bowl. The leader dipped twigs in the blood and then shook them, dispersing the blood while offering prayers for every participant in the ritual. The entire building structure was sprayed with this blood as well.

Norse pagans in northern Iceland beheaded oxen as sacrifices at the Hofstaðir temple hall, and the rituals continued for several years. Analysis of the animal bones revealed that the most common tools used in the slaughter were swords or axes, with blows to the neck also occasionally being used. Whatever the technique, it was a sight to behold, primarily due to the blood spurting from the injury. The meat from any animal that the Norse pagans killed or sacrificed was consumed during feasts.

They would use headstones to boil these meats in sizable cooking pits. It is possible for this to occur outside or indoors. Beer and mead (mjöð) drinking was a big part of the festivities. The chieftain was usually in charge of supplying the feasts, the ale, and all the meat needed for the sacrifice. Blótzveizla was the name given to this type of feast by Norse pagans.

Upon describing the Thrándheimr farmers, Snorri stated that the chief and his employees were in charge of bringing supplies to the Temple and executing the sacrifices. Norse pagans covered the Temple altar and the participants in the sacrifice with animal entrails because they thought the blood of the sacrificed animal had magical properties. In addition, a sacrificial cup was consecrated by the chieftain while it was being passed over the fire. In order to thank Odin for helping them win the war, Norse pagans raised a glass of beer to him. They also raised a glass to Njörðr and Freya for peace and a bountiful harvest. At the Jól, til árs ok friðar celebrations, a similar toast was made to the gods in appreciation of fertility, peace, and a bountiful harvest. The old religion and its customs included a variety of sacrificial feasts (blótveizlur, blótdrykkjur) among the Scandinavians. These customs gained popularity among a wide range of non-Norse pagans. Several of these customs were quickly incorporated into other celebrations, and many of the antiquated customs are still evident in regular Nordic festivals today.

Sigvatr Þórðarson, a Norwegian skald, wrote a poem in the eleventh century describing álfablót and other related family rites that the Norse pagans performed in western Sweden. These customs, however, were limited to family members and were performed on farm homesteads. Some Nordic customs were eventually observed being carried out by outsiders. Helgi, the Icelandic skald, claims that Trausti spoke of a slain enemy that he had sacrificed to Odin.

The saga of Ásmundar berserkjabana and Orkneyinga describes another instance of captured enemies being offered as sacrifices to Odin. The sacrificial bodies were apparently young females whose prior bone injuries had healed, based on remains discovered near Uppaland. ..It might have been an indication of Norse paganism, or it might have been a coincidence with the sacrifices made with war prisoners as the written corpus describes them.

Norse Pagan texts ascribed human sacrifices to Odin in all cases and in everything pertaining to him. But in the eyes of the Norse pagans, human life was the ultimate acceptable sacrifice for placating their gods or goddesses. Written records indicate that Odin, the king among the gods, asked for sacrifices made of human blood, or that his adherents were more adamant about making the greatest sacrifice possible for their monarch god. In any case, more human sacrifices are said to have been offered to Odin than to any other Norse god.

Ritual passage

The Old Norse ausa vatni, or water sprinkling ritual, was described as the means by which a child was welcomed into a family in the Eddic poems "Rígslula" and "Hávamál." The child was then given his name. Still, infants were only given names that honor departed family members. This is because, especially within the family, they held a strong belief in the custom of rebirth. Certain ancient Norse pagan texts claim that it also included explanations of the adoption rites. As per the Norwegian Gulaþing Law, the adoptive father was instructed to wear a leather shoe meant for this particular use. Then all other relatives were instructed to follow suit, including the adopted child. This involved them standing on the ground beneath a jarðarmen, a specially cut strip of grass, as part of a blood brotherhood ritual.

Norse pagans also performed family weddings in Iceland, complete with rituals. The Old Norse term for "bride run," which denotes that the bride was taken, is described by the Germanic word brúðhlaup. Nonetheless, the word has been interpreted differently by some academics. Jan de Vries was one of those, arguing that the word was meant to refer to a ritual in which the bride's family gave her to her new husband. Some literary sources assert that Thor and Frey were connected to nuptials, and Norse pagans were reported to have sacrificed to Frico—who was believed to be Freyr—during a marriage. In his account of Uppsala, Adam of Bremen described this.

According to the Eddaic poem "Þrymskviða," Thor once took his powerful hammer, Mjolnir, from his own lap while he was disguised. The hammer had been placed there during the ceremonial consecration of a marriage. Furthermore, according to "Þrymskviða," goddess Var was mentioned as one who blessed marriages. Snorri Sturluson claims in Gylfaginning that she heard men and women exchange vows. Her name Var means "beloved," and its etymology is linked to the Old Norse pagan religion of várar, or "vows." In Norse pagan religion, entombing the deceased was considered a symbolic act of passage. Archaeological evidence indicates that burial practices were carried out in both temporal and spatial dimensions. There appears to be no set funeral rite doctrine among Norse pagans, based on the stark differences in their practices. Cremations and inhumations had been commonplace among the Scandinavians throughout history. However, inhumations were also practiced in Iceland during the Viking era. They didn't cremate the dead, maybe one exception. In this era and area, almost everyone who passed away was interred in pits. Some of the remains were found in stone casts, boats, chambers, coffins, and similar locations. Researchers have discovered that some remains were scattered across the bottom of a pit, some were buried in kegs or pots, and some were found cremated next to a funeral pyre. No single grave has ever been discovered, despite the fact that numerous burials were discovered to have occurred in cemeteries. While some tombs were discovered in burial mounds or with a standing stone serving as a memorial, many other graves were unmarked.

CHAPTER FOUR
NORSE SHAMANISM

Shamanism is a system of religious practice that was part of Norse Pagan religion. Shamanism was merely a religious system among the Norse pagans, and it's still one of the most common ones today. There was, it was felt by many, a close relationship between these religious practices and those of indigenous and tribal societies. This is coupled with a strong conviction that individuals who practiced this religion possessed extraordinary abilities that allowed them to communicate with the spiritual or invisible world. Norse pagans think shamans are strong enough to communicate with spirits and heal a wide range of illnesses.

Additionally, they think that shamans have the ability to transport deceased people's souls to either the hereafter or the place they are being sent. Many Norse pagans around the world still regard shamanism, which has its roots in various regions of Asia and Northern Europe, to be a deeply religious practice. Changes brought about by imperialism and colonialism made many people less inclined to accept or even engage in traditional spiritualist practices. However, many communities are not only embracing it but also occasionally practicing it thanks to the reclaiming of self-determination and dynamic traditions.

Some were unaffected by the consequences and obstacles brought about by their isolation, even though colonialism and imperialism appeared to be a deterrent for some. For instance, the nomadic Tuvans, a tribe of survivors numbering over 2,500, were one of the most remote Russian tribes and an isolated group whose shamanic practices were untouched by imperialism and colonialism. Because of their remote existence, these people had been disregarded, which explains why modern religions haven't been able to have any impact on them.

Norse pagans around the world have differing opinions regarding the religion of shamanism. In spite of this, there were still some aspects of shamanism that all Norse pagans agreed upon.

Below is a list of common beliefs Eliade holds regarding Shamanism.

There are spirits. They are important to society and people's lives; they don't just exist for themselves.

They can harm people while at the same time bringing good fortune and luck to others.

Shamans hold the key to communicating with the spirit world.

A person suffering from one of the many illnesses brought on by evil spirits can be cured by shamans.

Shamans employ methods to bring about a trance before embarking on a vision quest and to promote ecstasy during a vision.

The spirit of a shaman can transcend beyond the physical realm and delve into the paranormal realm in search of solutions to challenges that appear insurmountable.

Shamans possess the ability to summon images of animals that they believe to be messengers, spirit guides, or omens.

Shamans are skilled in a variety of divination techniques, including scrying, runes, and bone throwing. They might also be able to predict what lies ahead.

Eliade's shaman conceptualization, according to Alice Kehoe's notes, creates an image of an indigenous culture that is Universalist and perpetuates ideas of an Indian who died (or was dying) and a noble savage. Through their practice of Shamanism, Norse pagans hold the belief that the physical world we inhabit is under the power of the unseen realm. It's also thought that the physical world is ruled by ghosts. These people think it's challenging to identify the underlying cause of illnesses or diseases. They held that the spiritual realm—which includes both evil and good spirits—is the source of the causes. Because of this, people frequently employ both medical and spiritual treatments to cure or treat a variety of illnesses.

Typically, a shaman enters the body of an ill person to battle spiritual ailments and heals them by chasing or expelling the contagious spirit.

Since many shamans are well-versed in the uses of locally grown medicinal plants, which includes both historical and contemporary practices, the majority of them recommend herbal remedies or cures for patients. In certain places, shamans gain direct knowledge from the plants themselves, utilizing their effects and the inherent healing qualities of each one. This will only take place if the patron spirits who reside in those plants have given them permission. Shamans in the Peruvian Amazon region invoke spirits with medicine songs, or icaros. A spirit's medicine song must be completely understood by the shaman before the spirit can be called forth. A totem is a popular tool for spirit summoning because it is thought to be very strong and to possess the spirit of animation.

We have to presume that these methods were widely employed in antiquity. During those times, people found that there were more benefits associated with "carefully listening and paying attention to what stones and the oak would say, believing that these objects speak nothing but the truth." Sorcery or witchcraft is known as brujería in Latin America, and it is said to exist in many global societies. Plato wrote in his Phaedrus that "the first prophecies were the words of an oak." Some societies hold the view that shamans are omnipotent, capable of curing any illness, and that they can kill anyone, whenever they please. People who are knowledgeable about shamanic practices are frequently regarded as strong members of their communities and hold prominent roles. People might, however, view them as capable of causing possible harm to others out of suspicion or fear.

A shaman who practices shamanism is subject to significant personal risk. Exposure to the plants that the shamans used is one way to illustrate this. If a shaman uses them incorrectly, this exposure may occasionally be poisonous or lethal. Shamans use spells to protect themselves from these deadly consequences or related risks; as a result, harmful plants are ritualized before being used by shamans.

Shamanism and Odin

In the earliest primary sources of information about Germanic ways before the Christian era, Norse pagans frequently depict Odin, the head of the gods, as the epitome of a shamanic figure. "Odin" (Old Norse Óðinn), as the name implies, is a compound word made up of the words óðr, which means "ecstasy, fury, inspiration," and "-inn," which is a suffix and is regarded as a definite masculine article. In terms of Odin's name, it translates as "The Master of Ecstasy." This was confirmed by the 11th-century historian Adam of Bremen, who translated the name of the Norse pagan god Odin as meaning "The Furious." This translation links Odin to "ecstatic trance," one of the qualities that define a shaman. When placed at the end of a word, it often means something similar to "the master of" or "a perfect example."

The shamanic spiritual journeys of Odin are properly documented. The Ynglinga Saga's records indicate that Odin would "transit to faraway lands on his errands or those of others" as he readied others for death or sleep. An additional source of evidence comes from the Eddic poem "Baldur's Dreams," in which Odin, acting on behalf of his son, rides Sleipnir, an eight-legged horse associated with northern Eurasian Shamanism, to the otherworld or world beyond in order to consult with a deceased seeress.

Like all Shamans in the world, Odin was accompanied by many familiar spirits, the most notable of which were the two ravens, Huginn and Muninn. Shamans usually have to go through a ceremonial death and rebirth in order to gain the necessary abilities. When Odin found the runes, he experienced both death and rebirth. Odin became not only a very powerful god but also one of the most knowledgeable, wisest, and magically powerful beings in the universe after learning about the runes. It was thought that Odin practiced seidr, which he may have picked up from Freya, the goddess of Norse paganism.

Shaman in Religion, Magic, and Warrior

There were other forms of shamanism that were widely accepted and socially practiced. Totemistic warriors and elite bands were among the more common forms in Germanic society; some Warband warriors were reputed to have gone insane, primarily due to the fact that they were not viewed as regular or conventional soldiers. Certain aspects of these warriors' fighting styles, spiritual beliefs, and early ritual participation did make them "berserkers." The warriors were led and inspired by Odin, the same god who inspired the seidr-workers, and as a result of these practices, some of their followers referred to them as "warrior shamans." According to the Saga of Ynglinga, Odin's warriors could fight without the use of armor because they had the strength of bulls or bears and the ferocity of wolves or dogs, which caused them to bite the shields of the opponents they defeated.

Howling and foaming at the mouth, they would dash through the combative soldiers. Some wore animal pelts; others abandoned their armor and shields, trusting only in their craze to carry them through to victory. Several of the greatest fighters are never on the front lines. They remained in their tents and concentrated on the fight. Like enormous animals, spirit forms would prowl through the fighters, wreaking havoc and leaving casualties in their wake. It was said that one of Odin's most common ecstatic states was "going berserk." The warriors never put on their shields in these kinds of battle trances, suggesting a symbolic social persona. A totemic animal spirit seemed to be fully occupied by them. They sometimes even went so far as to transform into wolves or bears by shifting or changing their form.

Shamanic Rituals

Shamans, whenever they wished to effect a transition from consciousness, would traverse the axis Mundi, entering into the "spirit world," going into a state of blissful trance. This can be accomplished in a number of ways. They can use entheogens, rituals, or autohypnosis to enter the spirit world. There are many more methods for doing this, and they are frequently combined. A psychoactive drug known as an entheogen, or "generation of the divine within," has been incorporated into several religions, including Norse Paganism. Shamans enter the spirit world with this substance. They have also been used for thousands of years by numerous cultures, and they were also used in ritualistic settings.

Peyote, fly agaric (Amanita Muscaria), psilocybin, and other drugs were used by many cultures (including Norse pagans), while other drugs included raw tobacco, cannabis, iboga, Salvia divinorum, and ayahuasca. Psychoactive ingredients found in entheogenic plants have historically been applied to people going on spiritual pilgrimages. "Ayahuasca tourism" has grown in popularity as a result of the decades-long surge in tourism to Brazil, Peru, and other nations.

Songs and Music

Shamanism is regarded as varied in Norse paganism, with numerous related songs and musical compositions having their origins in various cultures. Onomatopoeia is used in some shamanic songs to mimic natural sounds, but it's important to note that sound mimesis isn't always associated with shamanism in other cultures. Other useful uses could include luring game during a hunt or providing entertainment for others (Inuit throat singing).

Beginning and Acquiring Knowledge

Shamans claimed that in Norse paganism, one could not simply be a shaman without going through certain procedures. This led to a situation where some claimed they inherited their powers, while others claimed their calling came from specific signs or dreams. In traditional societies, becoming a shaman takes a long time—at least a year, and frequently much longer. A rite of passage for individuals aspiring to become shamans, the "shamanic initiatory crisis" was a Norse religious phenomenon that Turner and his colleagues discussed. A crisis or illness related to a psychological disorder was the main focus of the rite.

Other Shamanic Traditions

Ecstatic dance

Vigils or night watches

Mariri

Ayahuasca rituals

Abstinence

Songs about Icaros and medicine

An initiatory illness-affected training shaman feels that this is not an isolated incident. The significance of the initial illness, however, has to do with Chuonnasuan, one of Northeast China's last Tungus shamans. The wounded healer was revered as the embodiment of the struggles and path of a shaman. For two main reasons, those who aspired to become shamans endured this illness that nearly brought them to their demise. To begin with, this is the Shaman's journey to the afterlife or underworld. The shaman can descend into the underworld to heal the sick and discover knowledge that will benefit his tribe when he makes the journey there. Furthermore, it is said that a shaman must become ill in order to comprehend the illness; upon recovering from the illness, they are endowed with the ability to cure anyone who is ill.

CHAPTER FIVE
NORSE DEITIES AND GODS

The gods that the Norse pagans greatly revered were numerous. All these gods, though, had unique roles and abilities. The majority of these gods are still revered today, even with the advent of Christianity and other world religions. Some of them are thought to even show up in the things we do. For instance, the name Thursday appears to be associated with the god Thor.

(Woden's day) and Odin, who is also Woden, as observed on Wednesday. According to Norse mythology, there was a bottomless chasm called Ginnugagap before time began. Niflheim, the Land of Ice, and Muspelheim, the Land of Fire, are divided by Ginnugagap. Due to the combined might of the two countries, a battle broke out, and the blazing cold dissolved into droplets of water that eventually became living things.

The giant and hermaphrodite Ymir was the first human, formed by the water droplets but killed by Odin and his brothers. Vè, Vili, and Odin were Ymir's descendants, and they used his body—including his skull, brains, teeth, and flesh—to construct a world of Nordic mythology.

The Norse Gods

The gods are divided into the Vanir and Æsir clans. Tyr, Baldr, Frigg, Thor, Odin, Loki, Heimdall, and Hod were among the gods of the Çsir. All other Norse gods are most in awe of and elevated toward this god or group of gods. In Norse mythology, they are also referred to as the principal gods.

The fertility gods were among the Vanir, chief among them being Freyr, Freyja, and Nj ɫ rðr. The two clans decided it was better to unite, pooling their ideals and powers to guarantee a prosperous life for their people, despite the gods' intense animosity toward one another. Several gods from Norse mythology were worshipped by Norse pagans in the Scandinavian North. Nonetheless, we now know more about the existence of the majority of these gods and how the Norse pagans perceived them in their worship thanks to a few old texts and archeological discoveries.

The impact of the Middle Ages on Norse religion is evident in many instances. The best of them, though, are related to Vanir's narration of the Æsir war. This instance occurred when two distinct god clans—representatives of the Æsir and Vanir tribes of Norse gods—joined forces to complete a single mission. These are a few of the most significant Norse gods and goddesses that you should be aware of.

Ymir

One of the most significant gods in Norse mythology was Ymir, who was known as the ancestor of the giant god. Ymir, the first and earliest ancestor of all jötnar (mythological personalities that ranged from giants to different unique beings), is one of the early gods of this mythology, just like the myths of the Egyptians and the Mesopotamians. The giants' god Ymir is thought to have been the "earliest human," in contrast to a very strict classification as one of the many other Norse gods. It is thought that Ymir was formed from Niflheim ice and Muspelheim fire, long before Earth was formed. Ymir was a hermaphrodite, meaning he possessed both male and female reproductive organs. As such, he was the father of all future generations of beings. Ymir was a role model for other Norse gods of antiquity, but his story took a turn when he became the first person to meet a terrible end due to his malevolent manipulations. Consequently, Buri, the second creature among the Norse gods after Ymir and sometimes regarded as the first, had a son named Bor. Bor wed Bestla, a descendant of the Ymir. Odin, Vili, and Ve are the names of Buri's three sons from her marriage to Bustle. Ymir challenged the young gods out of frustration and rage, which led to his brother killing him. The young Norse gods used the giant's corpse to create Earth after

Ymir died. His bones formed the mountains and rocks, and his blood formed the oceans and seas. His skull became the sky and the heavens, and his hair was used to make trees. Clouds were formed by Ymir's brain, and Midgard was formed by his eyebrows.

The most powerful of the Aesir gods, Odin

Among several other gods, Odin—also referred to as Óðinn in Norse mythology and the king of the Aesir gods—remains the most worshipped deity in Norse paganism. Of all the Norse gods, Odin was the most enigmatic, though. The king gods of Aesir held him in the highest regard. The belief that Odin held a prominent position in the mythology of the Germanic gods' dates back to Tacitus' Germania, written in the late first century AD. In this work, the King of Aesir gods is regarded as having the same status as the Roman god Mercury. Due to the legendary abilities and superiority of the Aesir gods over those with Germanic ancestry, he had strong ties to various, occasionally opposing facets. And among these facets of his notoriety are death, wisdom, healing, sorcery, and more.

The Aesir god Odin had a contradictory aspect when it came to his wisdom, which caused people to depict him as a gaunt wanderer. The latter never got tired of being the king of Asgard and searching for knowledge. One tale exemplifies Odin's zeal or willingness to seek out wisdom and knowledge in order to learn more. That was the tale of the time he selflessly gouged out an eye to give to Mimir. Due to his consumption of water from the Urd well, Mimir was regarded as a mysterious being possessing unparalleled knowledge and insight. Mimir gave the Aesir god Odin water from the well at the base of Yggdrasil after his eye was gouged out. (Yggdrasil was a cosmic tree that connected the nine worlds of mythology).

Despite having given up his eye to drink from the well, his intimidating appearance made him seem as strong as the god of war. His personality was pure chaos and battle fever; it was the part of him that prioritized the berserkers and warlords over everyone else. Even now, Wednesday (also known as Woden's Day) is one of the days of the week on which his name is still connected. In Old English, Odin was called Wöden, and in Old German, Wotan.

The Queen of the Aesir Gods, Frigg

In the Pantheon, Frigg was the goddess of the sky and the queen of the Aesir. She was unique since she was married to Odin and had connections to marriage, fertility, families, and other domestic issues due to her extensive knowledge. Because of her love for her family, the Aesir Queen was regarded as a mythical figure among the Norse gods and was associated with happiness and family life. But this side of the goddess resulted in the tragedy involving Baldr, her favorite and most beloved child. The most unexpected aspect is how mysterious her Ancient Germanic version is, even though she is well-known in more recent Norse mythology (this was the Viking era). Many academics continue to debate this issue today. The Queen of the Aesir goddess, Frigg, was identified with Freyja in the protogermanic era according to one origin-based hypothesis. The name "Friday" comes from the name of the sky goddess, Frigg.

Thor

Among the gods of Norse mythology, Thor was the most well-liked and devoted protector of Asgard. Thor, also called Þórr in Old Norse, was a powerful and boisterous character. Because of this, he was held in high regard by the early Middle Ages Germanic people as a great warrior of noble status. The Aesir god Odin and his wife Fjörgyn (not to be confused with Frigg) were the parents of Thor. He was represented as having red eyes and a beard. When it came to protecting the Aesir's Asgard stronghold, Thor was known for being a devoted and trustworthy warrior. But this implied that his identity as a warrior was to defend the universe's order.

When it came to strength, no other god could match Thor. He is still the strongest of all the gods and creatures from Norse mythology, according to Poetic Edda. Even though Thor was extraordinarily strong, he enhanced his strength with specially designed tools. Iron gloves and a Megingjard belt, known as megingjarëar, were among those tools.

Thor, the devoted protector of Asgard, was one of the most revered gods in Norse mythology because of his numerous attributes and strength. But one thing that he had in common with his personality was his hammer, Mjöllnir, which means roughly "lightning" and was made for him by a dwarf. This hammer alluded to thunder perception subtly. He rode out in his chariots and used this hammer, which made it famous, to slay giants. He was distinguished by the fact that his chariot was drawn by two enormous goats. Tanngniost and Tanngrisnir were the goats' given names.

The fact that Thor was revered as the god of agriculture was just another incredible quality about him. The god of hallowing and fertility, Thor, also had a connection to this. As a sky god, Thor was thought to be able to create rain, which is why he was revered as the god of agriculture. In addition, Thor was wed to Sif, a goddess representing the fields of crops, particularly grain crops, and possessing the softest, longest golden hair.

Nonetheless, Thor and his spouse had a successful marriage. The god Thor is frequently reflected in a contemporary setting. Thursday, the fifth day of the week, is derived from the Old English word Íurresdæg. It is a contraction of Íunresdæg, which literally translates to "Thor's day," and may have been influenced by the Old Norse word Íorsdagr.

Balder

Balder, the god of purity and light, was the younger son of Odin and Frigg. The bright summer sun was Balder, also known as Baldur (Baldr in the Old Norse religion), the half-brother of the most powerful god, Thor. Balder was highly revered by Norse pagans, who saw him as a just and fair god. Baldr was revered as a gracious, sage, and divine being who was more beautiful than the most exquisite flowers. Built to match his own beauty, he lived in a magnificent hall that was regarded as the most exquisite of all the halls of the Norse gods. The hall was made of gilded silver and had ornate pillars. It was situated in Breidablik, Asgard. But only the purest of hearts were allowed entry into this exquisite hall.

Balder owned Hringhorn, the greatest ship ever built. He used the ship as a funeral pyre. Concerning the tragedy of Balder's demise, it should be noted that Höðr, Balder's twin brother, contributed to his demise, albeit unintentionally. Höðr received a mistletoe dart from the crafty and mischievous god Loki. Except for mistletoe, Loki was aware that no living thing in Asgard or Midgard could hurt Baldr.

After his passing, Balder's notoriety grew even more. Although many believed the god of light and purity to be eternal, a prophecy had already predicted his demise. Balder's mother, Frigg, went to every person in the universe to swear an oath that none of them would harm Balder in order to prevent the prophecy from coming true. But among all the things Frigg visited, she spared the mistletoe because she thought it was too small and too dangerous to endanger Balder's life.

In actuality, Loki capitalized on Balder's error, which prompted the cunning god to fashion an arrow from mistletoe. Balder's half-brother Höðr started hurling the dart straight at him, as was customary among the Norse gods. As the dart entered the "best of the gods'" heart, the expected outcome was that the dart would either fall off or bounce back, but instead the man died. Many Norse gods were so overcome with grief as a result that they tried to bring the god of light and purity back to life. The gods' efforts were in vain since Balder was already headed for Hell. Due to the cruel prank of the cunning Loki, one of the best gods among the Norse gods was lost.

Vidar, the Quiet God of Retribution

Grid (or Gríðr), the son of the jötunn, and Odin's son Vidar are depicted as the silent god of vengeance. Known by another name in the past, Víðarr, the Poetic Edda contains an attestation of his name. Strongly symbolic of retribution, this predicted how Vidar would exact revenge at Ragnarok on Odin, the man who killed his father. One of the primary Norse gods who would survive the decisive conflict was Vidar, who "would live on the Idavoll field after the battle."

According to the Gylfannong, the first part of the Poetic Edda, Vidar knew he would have to wear heavy shoes like Thor did and that he would have to mend them all the time. Since these shoes would comparatively protect the god's feet, Vidar wore them. To break the monster's heart, he put his foot on Fenrir's throat. It's important to remember that Völuspá told how Fenrir would be killed by the silent god of vengeance thrusting his sword into the wolf's heart. Because of this, it became a religious custom for Norse shoemakers to save small pieces of leather from their shoe trimmings as a means of maintaining a spiritual bond with the vengeful, silent god.

The silent quality of the Vidar might have been related to the vengeance ritual, which involved putting warriors through a period of silence as a means of focus or as a component of purification rites. The mute god of retaliation possessed strength that was even greater than that of Thor. But Vidar did not have the fiery temperament or high spirits of his famous half-brother. Georges Dumézil postulated that the god of vengeance originated as an Indo-European deity, based on historical and etymological evidence. This god was preoccupied with space, just like the Hindu mythological figure Vishnu was.

Tyr, the God of War

Tyr was the god of war and valorous conquest. Numerous Norse pagans held him in high regard due to his bravery, making him the most fearless of all the Norse gods. Tyr was closely associated with war, particularly with the protocol of hostilities and agreements. Before Odin took his place, Tyr—who had a mysterious beginning—was regarded as the most significant and oldest of the Germanic people's ancient Norse gods. According to some myths, Tyr was the son of Odin, but according to others, he was the son of a giant named Hymir. Norse pagans also considered Tyr to be the god of justice and oaths because of his association with formalities. Tyr was portrayed as having only one hand since the gods attempted to bind the giant wolf Fenrir and he lost the other. Tyr's offering meant that until Ragnarok, Fenrir would be enchantedly chained to a boulder. Based on the Ragnarok's prone version, the god of vengeance was said to have died when Garm, a guard of the door to Hel, slew him in opposition to Fenrir, despite his strength (as demonstrated by holding the monstrous wolf Fenrir bound). Tyr, the god of vengeance and oaths, is significant in a modern sense, much as some other Norse gods are. The Old English name Tiw (a variation of the god's name) was closely associated with the Roman god Mars. Furthermore, Marti, or Mars's Day, gave rise to tiwesdæg, or Tuesday.

Bragi

As a skaldic God in Norse mythology, Bragi was revered. Bragi, also called the "Bard," was an Asgardian god; a rough translation of Bragi is "poet." Bragi was linked to a legendary individual who shared traits with the real-life bard Bragi Boddason from the ninth century. Boddason himself is thought to have been a member of Björn and Ragnar Ladbrok's court at Hauge. Whatever the truth, Bragi, the skaldic god, was considered the bard of Valhalla, Odin's mighty heaven and hall, where all fallen warriors and heroes await their final meeting at Ragnarok. This is how the legends depicted him. The fallen warriors that the Valkyrie brought to Odin's hall, the Einherjar hordes, delighted and sang Bragi, who was worshipped as a poet-god. Among the few names mentioned in the Poetic Edda was Bragi Boddason, despite having some historical counterparts. Other names were Bragi Högnason, who was mentioned in the Helgakviða Hundingsbana, and Bragi, son of Hálfdan, as mentioned in Skjáldskaparmál.

Idun

A female deity from Norse mythology was called Idun. The young goddess of rejuvenation, known as Iðunn, which translates to "Rejuvenating One," belonged to the Aesir tribe of the Norse gods. In Norse mythology, Idun was revered as the goddess of eternal youth. Idun's remarkably flamboyantly golden long hair served as a representation of her youth. As per mythological storytelling, Bragi, the Asgardian poet, was the spouse of the goddess of youth. Aside from her physical characteristics, Idun was thought to possess latent powers, which made her much more fascinating to mythology enthusiasts.

It was thought that the goddess of youth possessed fruit, sometimes called apples. The Edda Prose and Haustlöng both mention the belief that these fruits bestowed upon their bearers the gift of immortality. In essence, these served as the "fuels" that allowed the inhabitants of Asgard to live forever. As a result, Idun rose to prominence within the Norse pantheon of gods. Another unpopular myth about Idun has her being accused of cheating by none other than the crafty and mischievous trickster god, Loki. However, a lack of sufficient sources means that the outcome of these particular allegations is still unknown.

Loki

The demise of the god of purity and light is always remembered when the name of the cunning deity Loki is mentioned. In mythology, Loki was associated with being crafty and mischievous. Among other gods, the Egyptian god Set was likened to Loki in terms of their craftiness. He was a jötunn, the son of the giant Farbauti and the goddess Laufey, the giantess's wife. They were also capable of changing their shape.

In general, Loki was regarded as a god with good intentions despite his capricious schemes. But Loki was thought to be crafty and the catalyst for a number of heinous deeds. Some of which were associated with unfavorable incidents, misfortunes, and tragedies, like the one that resulted in the demise of Balder, the god of purity and light. Being an outsider among the Aesir gods was one of Loki's greatest attributes. He was called a cunning god, but that might have just been a plot about him involving the other gods. One of the best illustrations of Loki's complex relationships with the other Norse gods is the one between Thor and Loki. A tale known as "Lokasenns," or "Loki's Quarrel," from the Poetic Edda claims that after insulting the Hammer god, Loki was forced to hide out of fear of Mjolnir, Thor's formidable hammer.

In Þrymskviða, also known as Thrymskvida in English, Loki and Thor, the gods, maintained a cordial and amicable friendship. On the other hand, this fellowship saw their scheme to take the lost Mjölnir from the jötunn Þrymr. It is well known that Loki had a complicated backstory and persona. Nevertheless, there had been prophecies that he would be a conduit for the end of several Norse gods during Ragnarok. One such prophecy stated that Fenrir, the wolf son of Loki, would kill Odin. The other son of Loki, Jörmungandr, the Serpent, would also poison the hammer god Thor, causing him to die accordingly.

CHAPTER SIX

THE UNDERWORLD'S ALMIGHTY – HELL

Here comes Hel, the ruler of the underworld, another significant figure in Norse mythology. When we hear the name Hel, we frequently associate it with the realm of punishment and unending condemnation. With a diverse population that included Jörmungandr the serpent and Fenrir the wolf, two of Loki's offspring, its Germanic side was not without difficulty. Other residents of Hel (also referred to as Helheim) passed away from illness or old age. Hel was one of Loki's children. Angrboda, a giantess, was her mother. It is thought that Hel chose the destiny for every soul that was transported to her world.

Numerous Viking sagas and poems made reference to Hel; in many of them, she was portrayed as having a somewhat lifeless face. They also depicted her with the thighs and legs of a corpse and the body of a living woman. Though she may have had a terrible or terrifying appearance, Hel was one of the most potent Norse goddesses. Within her domain, Hel was so strong that even the god Odin of the Aesir could not stand against her. The untimely demise of Balder validated Hel's influence and her connection to Lowe. Among the other Norse Aesir gods, she was the one who gathered the greatest amount of wisdom and the purest hearts; she would be the judge who would decide when the god would end.

The Watchful Keeper of Asgard – Heimdall

Heimdall was revered as the stronghold of the Aesir Norse gods and Asgard's watchful protector. The stronghold god was considered to be the giant Fornjót descendant Ægir, the grandson of the sea jötunn (Jötnar's singular). Gjallarhorn, or the "Resounding Horn," is the horn that always represents Heimdall (also known as Heimdallr in Old Norse). When an intruder approached the home of the Æsir tribe of gods, this horn was used to punish them. When it came to Heimdall's duty of "guarding," the watchful god possessed extraordinary hearing and sharp eyesight that allowed him to see for hundreds of miles. In addition, Heimdall possessed an abundance of energy and historical knowledge.

According to certain myths, Heimdallr, Asgard's watchful protector, might have been the ancestor of all people. This was based on hazy references found in the Völuspá poem, an Old Norse poem. Other theories put forth by some academics indicated that it demonstrated how the figurehead guardian god was once thought of by Norse pagans as the one who created human classes and hierarchy. In terms of mythology, Heimdall was also a major factor in Ragnarok's downfall. Some people think that the god would go to a certain location and sound the Gjallarhorn to announce the arrival of the giants and other monsters. It was predicted that in the ensuing conflict, Loki and Heimdallr would murder one another.

Njord, the God of Wealth and Seas

The god of wealth and the seas, Njord, would have to be included in any list of Norse gods. Njord, also known as Njörðr, belonged to the Vanir branch of Norse gods. But when their world ended, Njord was later admitted as one of the Aesir. According to myth, the Norse pagans revered Njord, also known as Nyord, as a significant maritime deity. He was associated with fertility and the seas. Among the Germanic people, Njord might have been considered the "richest" divine god among the other Norse mythological deities. In reference to the original sea god and wealth myth, this was associated with Njord's marriage to the giantess Skadi. When Skadi saw Njord's legs and feet, she decided to marry him because she had mistaken them for Baldr's and believed that was the man she was marrying.

The couple's home life was miserable as a result. The giantess Skadi had always been excited to spend time at her home in the snow-capped mountains, so their union was not as happy as she had imagined. Her husband, however, liked to spend his time at his heavenly home, Nóatún, which means "The Place of

Ships." The seafaring god and the giantess parted ways eventually, as was to be expected. They did, however, embrace the arrival of their twins, the prominent Norse deities Freyr and Freya.

Freyr

Considered the fertility god, Freyr was one of the twins of Njord and Skaldic, the giantess. Among other Norse people, Freya—the twin sister of Freyr—was regarded as one of the most adored and respected. Being a member of the Vanir tribe of Norse gods, who opposed the Aesir, gave Freyr a distinct origin. Freyr was usually portrayed as a muscular man with long hair. Among the Norse pagans, the fertility god Freyr was celebrated as the primary deity of infertility. This was equivalent to fertility in terms of agriculture, sexuality, and ecology. It has been said that Freyr represents a bountiful harvest, tranquility, prosperity, and even manliness. These traits all represented Gullinborsti, or "Golden-Bristled," the boar of Freyr.

The son of the Skaldic giantess was the most beloved god of the Norse pagans because of his connection to these important pathways. When it came to marriage customs and harvest festivals, they revered and worshipped him. In this instance, a boar was sacrificed in order to kick off the festivities. The fertility god was symbolically associated with the boar. Norse mythology thus noted that the fertility god Freyr was reported to ride in chariots drawn by boars. As a result, priests from Germany formed processions and used chariots decorated with images of the fertility god to reenact travel. They took this action to symbolize that peace and prosperity would soon return to some parts of Germania.

Because the fertility god resided in Alfheim, the home of the elves, he was also connected to the elves. According to some academics, the god might have actually been the affluent king of these elves. Few materials, mainly historical sources and Norse folklore, support this assertion, though. In addition, the Norse god possessed a ship called Skíðblaðnir that had incredible features, the highly sought-after capacity to always have favorable wind, and a "modular" design that allowed the desirable ship to be folded up into a very small size.

Freya

Similar to Freyr, her twin brother Freya, who was originally a member of the Norse deity tribe and was translated as "Lady" in Old Norse religion. After the tribal war was over, Freya—also known as the goddess of fate and destiny—became an honorary and devoted member of the Aesir. Freya has stood for all things beautiful, all facets of love, and even all things luxurious. Another depiction of Freya was that of a sensual goddess who cherished adventure. The goddess of fate and destiny represented völva, also known as anglicized vala. It is said that the female Norse seer possessed the ability to use seidr, a type of magic connected to fate.

It was believed that Freya, the goddess of destiny, could control and change people's wishes and fortunes as she pleased. Freya was once thought of as a goddess possessing the indiscernible demeanor of a cat. Freya was considered, along with other goddesses from Norse mythology, to be the ruler of Folkvang, the afterlife. This gave her the opportunity to select the warriors she desired from those who lost their lives in battle, with the Valkyries carrying the remaining warriors to Valhalla (see Bragi for further information).

This portrayal of a powerful volva was as accurate as possible in capturing the atmosphere of the Germanic pantheon, particularly in the 400–800 AD "Migration Period," or Völkerwanderung. The tribal societies represented by the chieftain warrior, who would lead them in plunder and combat, and his wife, a prophetess who used magic to ensure the outcome of these battles was in their favor, were of great benefit to the two gods at the head of the pantheon.

Some academics and historians contend that Odin and Frigg, sometimes known as the "Norse personalities," shared a common goal. Either Frigg was Freya but went by a different name, or she possessed the same traits as Freya. The Norse pagans believed that Óðinn, or Odin, was just óër with the suffix -inn added, while Óðr, which means "ecstasy" or "furor," was married to Freya.

Chapter 6: Legends of the Norse

According to the mythology and cosmology of the ancient Norse religion, Yggdrasil, the world tree, originated in the first Ginnungagap void and was an incredibly good tree. The nine worlds of Norse mythology were unified by the world tree Yggdrasil, and these worlds included:

Niflheim

Muspelheim

Asgar

Midgard

Jotunheim

Vanaheim

Alfheim

Svartalfheim

Hel

The three roots of the world tree Yggdrasil extended far into the sky, reaching the Mimisbrunnr well and the Hvergelmir spring. The Norns were a group of particular female personalities. These Norns were in charge of drawing water from Urðarbrunnr, the well, and spinning the threads of fate to cover the world tree. Some stags, including Duraþrór, Dvalinn, Dáinn, and Duneyrr, fed continuously on the world tree. But even though they kept eating Yggdrasil, their ability to grow didn't change because it still had the ability to heal and defend against the harsh realities of life. An eagle perched on the highest branch of the tree. The human world of Midgard Earth experienced wind when the eagle started to beat its wings. The great serpent Niðhūggr was gnawing at the base of Yggdrasil, its home being the foot of the world tree. Ratatoskr, the squirrel, was constantly on the move, sending out messages and insults.

At the center of the cosmos lay a sacred tree known as Yggdrasil, the world tree. As previously mentioned, the growth originated from the Ginnungagap void, which was bounded on one side by Muspelheim, the land of fire, and Niflheim, the realm of fog and mist. The gods Audhumla (the cow) and Ymir (the giant) were created when the ice of Niflheim, the world of mist and fog, began to melt due to the heat of Muspelheim. Ymir was killed by Odin, the god of the Aesir, who was regarded as the "father of all gods" because of the separate contributions that these two creatures made to the creation of Odin.

CHAPTER SEVEN
NINE REALMS

There were various beings living in each of the nine worlds' realms, such as the gods' and goddesses' home, Asgard. Or Jotunheim, the world of the giants. The most revered Aesir king, Odin, and his brothers used Ymir's body to create other worlds (apart from Muspelheim and Niflheim) in Norse mythology. This occurred when the universe was being created. Norse mythology's nine worlds, however, weren't created by accident. Nine was an important number in Norse mythology. Snorri Sturlusson's Edda's Poetic revealed some of the indicators. To mention a few, Odin, the god of the Aesir, spent nine days and nights hanging atop the world tree. In Norse mythology, the number nine also has special meaning for Heimdall, the watchful protector of Asgard, who had nine daughters. Lastly, Njord, the god of wealth and the seas, spends nine days with Skadi. These are the nine Norse mythological worlds.

The Nine Realms

1. Niflheim: The Land of Mist and Fog

According to Norse mythology, Niflheim, also known as the Mist Abode or the World of Mist, was the coldest and darkest place of them all. It was said to be one of the two realms created first, and the name came from the Old Norse word Niðavellir. The northern Ginnungagap region contained Niflheim. Hvergelmir, sometimes referred to as the "bubbling, boiling spring," is a misty and foggy place that is thought to be the oldest spring on Earth. The dragon Nidhug, also called Níðhöggr in Old Norse, was said to guard the Hvergelmir. The Hvergelmir spring was regarded by Norse pagans as the origin of the cold rivers and as having created Élivágar, the other eleven rivers.

All living things came from the Hvergelmir spring, and all living things would eventually return to it. Through the mountains, the Élivágar ran to the Ginnungagap plains, where it froze into a thick, solid layer of ice. As Yggdrasil grew, a third, massive root shot out from its body, reaching Niflheim and the Hvergelmir spring, where it drew water to survive.

2. The Sacred Land - Mount Everest

Another one of the nine realms of Norse mythology was Muspelheim, also referred to as the Land of Fire. The world, called "Múspellsheimr" in Old Norse, was created at the same time as Niflheim. On the other hand, Niflheim formed in the world's extreme south. Muspelheim was known for being extremely hot and ablaze with lava, sparks, soot, and flames. The burning hot place was the abode of fire giants and fire demons, with its ruler known as Surtr. Surtr was a sworn enemy of Aesir. This ruler would ride out with his flaming sword in his hands at Ragnarok when the world ended. At this time, the ruler would attack the home of Aesir gods, Asgard, turning it into a flaming inferno.

3. Asgard: Aesir's Abode

Asgard was where the Aesir lived and was ruled by Odin, the king, Frigg, the queen, Thor, one of Asgard's most loyal defenders, and many other gods highly respected in Norse mythology. Asgard was one of the more fertile realms and was also blessed with the wealth of gold and jewels, more so than any other realm. It was surrounded by a wall that was never completed, built by a stonemason whom the gods discovered was pretending to be Hrimthurs; Thor struck him down. Valhalla's hall of slain warriors was also located in Asgard, a very large hall where Odin and the slain warriors wined and dined. The warriors who died in combat were called the Einherjar, and they would line up with the other dead, showing their support for Odin and their readiness to fight with him at Ragnarok.

4. Midgard (The Earth)

Midgard, also known as Earth, was a realm inhabited by humans. Midgard was surrounded by water, an impassable sea where Jormungandr, the massive sea serpent, lived. Asgard's gods traveled through Bifrost to get to the Earth, a rainbow bridge of flames that led to Himinbjorg, where Heimdallr, Asgard's vigilant god, lived.

According to the Icelandic Eddas, Ragnarok will bring the end of Earth, a destructive battle signifying the end of the world. Jormungadr will rise from the water, his venom poisoning the sea and the land, and the sea will rise and crash against the land. And the final battle will happen at Vígríðr plains. Virtually all living things will be destroyed, sinking below the water around Midgard, but the destruction will bring a new Midgard to life, a fertile, green land born of Ragnarok's hell.

5. Jotunheim: The Giants' Abode

Jotunheim ("Jötunheimr") was the world dedicated to the Giants (Jötnar). The giants were the chief enemies of the Aesir. This specific world of giants was made up of rocks, wilderness, and dense forests, lying in the snowy region on the ocean's outermost shores. As a result, the giants were mostly dependent on fish from the waters and forest animals. This was because of the absence of fertile lands in the world of the giants. There had always been a constant tussle between the giants and the Aesir.

On the other hand, they also shared affectionate moments. The Aesir King Odin, the hammer god Thor, and a few others were in love with people who were giants.

The trickster god Loki was also from the giant world of Jotunheim, but his acceptance in Aesir saw him live in Asgard until his punishment was accomplished. Jotunheim, the land of the giants, was separated from Asgard by the River Lving, a river that never froze. The Jotuns had their own version of Asgard, often known as Utgard, a stronghold so high that the top was rarely seen. Utgard's fortress was carved from blocks of snow and icicles, and this is where the Utgard king, Loki, lived.

6. Vanaheim: The Home of the Vanir

In Old Norse, Vanir was called Vanaheimr and was where the ancient Vanir gods lived. These gods were known to be masters of magic and sorcery. Norse pagans had high regard for them in Norse mythology due to their power to forecast what was to happen in the future. However, the exact location of the world of the Vanir gods and the description of what it looks like remains unknown to anyone. When the Aesir-Vanir war was over, several gods and goddesses were "gifted" to Asgard as a peace offering: Freya, Njord, Vanir, and Freyr.

7. Alfheim: The Light Elves' Abode

Alfheim was where the light elves dwelled and was located in heaven beside Asgard. According to Norse mythology, the light elves were incredibly beautiful, and Norse pagans called them "the guardian angels of Alfheim (Álfheimr or Ljósálfheimr in Old Norse.) The elves were considered the minor gods and creatures of nature and fertility. The fertility god Freyr was known as the ruler of this specific world. Light elves were powerful at helping or hindering the knowledge of humans using their magical powers. The light elves created great inspiration for poets in music and the arts.

8. Svartalfheim: The Dwarfs' Home

Translated as Svartálfaheimr or Niðavellir in the Old Norse religion, this was a home dedicated to dwarfs who took shelter beneath the rock, caves, and even underground at times. Hreidmar ruled this world up until his death. Svartalfheim was also referred to as the Dark fields. The dwarves could not be matched in their craftsmanship, and they gave many powerful items and gifts to the king, including Draupnir, a magical ring, and Odin's trusted spear, Gungnir.

9. Hel: The Dead Warriors' Home

Hel, also the same as "Helheim," was one of the nine worlds of Norse mythology. Hel was different from the hell described in Christianity, perceived as a place of torment in a world where many dead people and warriors would end up. Ruled by the Norse god called Hel, the underworld heaven in Norse mythology was more of a place where dead people would continue their lives but not a place where they would be tormented.

CHAPTER EIGHT
MONSTERS IN NORSE MYTHOLOGY

Norse mythology has various gods and goddess characters, and these characters were not the main powerful gods. However, many of these deities faced different creatures or monsters that continually challenged them and terrorized humans. There are many mythical stories in Norse mythology, ranging from the Aesir king gods Óðinn to the trickster god Loki.

Norse religion had existed for a long time, even before the arrival of the Christian religion. However, there was a decline in Norse paganism around a thousand years ago, with the Christian religion sweeping across every nook and cranny of northern Europe. Thanks to archeological discoveries and other reliable sources of information, with its amazingly fascinating stories, powerful gods and goddesses, and scary monsters, the Norse religion never lost its relevance and foothold.

Norse mythology included nine worlds, and each world was occupied by gods and goddesses worshipped by Norse pagans.

Also, each world had varieties of mythical monsters like elves, dwarfs, giants, and lots more. Norse mythology is mostly about its gods and goddesses. However, the Norse monsters flesh out the stories, challenging the supremacy of these deities and changing their destinies. There are many monsters in Norse mythology, with each having its role. Despite the long existence of these deities, we still have many of these creatures reflected in our daily lives, for example, woven into cultural wear. These monsters were of Norse mythology origin, and for people who do not understand, here are some of the Norse Paganism monsters and some of the worlds they belonged to.

Elves

Of the nine worlds, Alfheim, has been described as the home of elves under the rulership of the deity of fertility, Freyr. Elves were considered slim demi-gods, very tall, having pale hair and skin. Their beauty has been compared to the sun. Elves were not close to humans, keeping far from their affairs. However, this does not mean they had no relationship whatsoever with humans. Elves appeared to be human once in a while. When this happened, humans welcomed these monsters for two reasons, to cause illness or to cure it, depending on their mood. Being of a fluid race, elves did not subscribe to the usual human gender roles and were shown as having moral feelings toward humans. Some sources say that the monsters were two separate categories - Ljósálfar, the light elves termed as being "lighter than the sun," and Dökkálfar, the dark elves considered "blacker than pitch." Scholars dispute claims that the Dökkálfar was merely a way of bringing in the concept of good vs. evil or that they were simply dwarves but with a new name.

Draugar

This monster refers to the Norse mythology of the undead. Some stories say that the Draugar were blood-drinking monsters, but they were more like zombies than they were vampires. Draugar had the strength of a superhuman, allowing them to change to a bigger size at will. However, having the hideous looks of a dead body, the Draugar couldn't shake the unmistakable stench of decay. Commonly, these monsters were grave bound, being their home to secure and defend the treasures buried with them. However, Draugar has been known to invade communities to unleash mayhem on humans and punish people who have crossed their path in life.

Draugar were so powerful that they could kill an individual by crushing him with their superpowers. They didn't just kill humans but ate them even in their enlarged state. Indirectly, they could also kill by driving a person mad. They also manipulated their way into human dreams to torment them. When Draugar had finished tormenting their victims, they would not leave without leaving a sign to show that they had been responsible for the fate of their victims.

They had superpowers, but they could be killed by burning them, which shattered them, or they would decay excessively. One common belief is that malicious, evil, unpopular, or greedy people would transform into Draugar upon their death.

Dwarves

It was believed that Svartelheim was home to the black elves, also where the dwarves lived. However, modern misconceptions that dwarves were stout and short cannot be verified as nothing points to that being the case. Dwarves were termed "lesser creatures," which may have been where that misconception originated. The dwarves dwelled on Midgard, and Svartelheim was portrayed as an underground labyrinth of mines and forges. Dwarves had something that people referred to as special, and this was their smithing skill. Mjöllnir (Thor's hammer) remained one of the most amazing artifacts the dwarves forged. Also, these creatures forged Freyr's ship, always having favorable winds. Dwarves also forged the Aesir god Odin's ring and spear, Gungnir and Draupnir. These creatures had exceptional knowledge and wisdom. They were talented and magically powerful. In today's world, we also see four dwarves in geographical locations: Nordri, Austri, Sudri, and Vestri – West, South, North, and East. These dwarves are believed to have been the holders of the sky in the air by its corners, verifying how powerful they were.

Jormungandr

Jörmungandr, the same as the serpent of Midgard (Earth), was one of the offspring of Loki, the trickster god, and Angrboda. Jormungandr was a huge serpent that lived in the water around Midgard, or Earth, where the humans lived. Odin threw the serpent into the sea in a bid to stop him from causing trouble. However, he grew so big that he could encircle Earth, touching his tail with his mouth and creating a circle. It is believed that Jormungandr was an enemy of Thor and another story detailed an issue Thor had with Hymir, a Jotun fisherman. However, Thor was not pleased as the giant Hymir caught a whale in his favorite fishing location.

Thor insisted on heading out to sea, subsequently capturing Jormungandr on a hook. When he dragged the serpent out of the water, it dribbled venom and blood. This elicited such strong feelings in Hymir that he cut through the line before Thor could kill the serpent with Mjollnir, his mighty hammer, allowing Jormungandr to escape into the water. Some stories also claim that Jormungandr would rise from the sea during Ragnarok, poison the sky and the water, and that he and Thor were prophesied to kill one another. Jotnar

The Jotnar were considered giants in Norse mythology, possessing huge amounts of power that enabled them to compete with the Norse gods. Their name translates as "devourers," not referencing the giants' physical size in any way. They were not friends of the gods and represented calamity, the opposite of the order represented by the Asgard gods. Regardless of this, many gods from Asgard were descendants of the Jotnar. The Aesir king Odin was half Jotnar, and Thor was three-quarters Jotnar. Other gods in Asgard were not concerned with killing these monsters. However, their priority was to watch over them to keep the universe settled. In the Norse creation myth, where the cosmos was created from the body of the giant Ymir, Sheln is the universal balance role.

Fenrir

In Norse mythology, several wolves were mentioned, but the most famous among them all was Fenrir, the trickster god sired by Loki and the giantess Angrboda. Asgardian gods raised these creatures to prevent them from causing mayhem throughout the nine worlds. Fenrir grew fast, causing chaos wherever he went, and the gods saw that the only solution to stopping him was to chain him. The Asgard gods tricked him into being chained up by telling him the chains were a test of his strength. When Fenrir broke the chains with ease, the gods consulted with the elves, who then produced a magical chain that felt as light as a feather but could not be broken by anyone or anything.

Fenrir suspected the gods were trying to trick him, and he demanded a show of good faith if he let them chain him up. He demanded that a god put his hand into his giant mouth. Tyr, one of the gods, obliged even though he knew that it was a trick. Fenrir was chained to a boulder, and a sword was used to keep his jaws wide open. The drool from Fenrir's mouth formed Expectation, a foamy river mentioned in Ranganrok when Fenrir broke free of the chains and wreaked his revenge on the gods. It is also believed that Fenrir was the father of two other massive wolves, Hati and Skoll, said to have chased the moon and the sun across the sky. When the world ended, it was prophesied that Skoll would catch the sun and Hati would catch the moon, tearing them apart.

Fossegrimen

These creatures were also called the Grim. Fossegrimen were creatures of the water spirit. Their talent was used in playing the fiddle, emulating the sounds from the forest and the water and wind. When this creature taught the skill, Fossegrimen always requested an offering, specifically, a white goat thrown with the head turned away into a waterfall flowing to the north. As an alternative, smoked mutton could be offered to the creature on four consecutive Thursdays. The mutton would be stolen from a neighbor's storehouse. Not enough meat on the mutton bone was said to have led to the creature teaching a person only how to tune a fiddle, but if he were given enough, he would guide the person's right hand over the strews until they bled.

Ratatoskr

Yggdrasil, the world tree, was home to some creatures, one of whom was a squirrel called Ratatoskr. The squirrel's duty was to traverse the tree, delivering messages from the gods. Ratatoskr was considered mischievous and delightfully stirred up trouble between the hungry dragon living in Yggdrasil's roots and the eagle that sat at the top. Some stories say the squirrel had an ulterior motive, a sinister one, in making the eagle and the dragon come together to destroy the tree. Sleipnir

Here comes another one of the trickster god Loki's offspring, Sleipnir. This mighty 8-legged horse belonged to Odin. It was the best of his horses. Sleipnir was the offspring of the stallion Svaðilfari and the cunning Loki. Loki had pretended to be a mare and attempted to shift the attention of the owner of the stallion. The gods' messenger, Hermóðr, rode on this creature to

Hel to negotiate the release of Baldr when he died from the mistletoe strike by Höðr, his blind brother.

Huldra

The creatures were called the "wardens of the forest," and they belonged to the Ra group that protected multiple locations. They took female and male forms, with the latter being seen as beautiful, with great powers of seduction but with a bark-covered back and a cow's tail. They had the power to appear as young women, allowing them to explore the world of men, but their illusion could be broken if their tail was injured. In the form of females, the Huldra explored and lured young men back to the forest, where they would be forced into being what the Huldra wanted. At times, the Huldra would suck their victims dry, and any victim that escaped or who was freed had the power to live forever but would struggle to resist returning to their captors.

Mare

In Norse mythology, this creature was said to have been responsible for nightmares by sitting on a sleeping person. It was believed that Mare comprised the souls that left living people's bodies at night, like demons. These people were sometimes witches, and their souls were in an animal form, but often they were just normal people. It was also believed that young children would become the creature if their spirits wandered at night. It was also common for people to go wandering at night with their spirits, and one of the best examples of that was the Aesir king, Odin. He was so concerned that his wandering soul would one day not return to his body that he took to accompanying it. Norse pagans also believed that when the Mare monsters touched a person or animal's hair, it would tangle up. This explains a hair disease called Polish Plait, and it was often believed that a tree's roots would also become entangled if the Mare touched them. **Kraken**

These were creatures believed to live just off the shores of Norway and Greenland. Kraken was typically depicted as a huge creature of the sea, a massive squid or octopus-like monster. Some people say it was so big that people could be forgiven for thinking it was an island in the sea. However, it would sink if anyone reached the island, taking them with it. They had already set foot on it, and during the sinking process, the men would die, and their bodies became Kraken's meal. Norse pagans believed that when Kraken rose to the surface, it caused a large gulf or large body of running water that could be helpful to lay siege on ships. These creatures often fed on fish, luring fish to eat by releasing their excreta into the water. Their excreta was very thick and had a very strong odor, serving as bait to draw fish from near and far closer so that Kraken could eat them.

Norns

Norns in Norse mythology referred to female beings and creatures responsible for creating and controlling one's fate, including the fate of the gods. When an individual was born, norns showed up to weave their fatal thread by casting wooden lots. They also weaved a piece of cloth or carved signs into a piece of wood. According to Norse beliefs, their fate was sealed and could not be changed. There is no proof or corroboration that anyone ever met these creatures or had been able to change their fate. The three major Norns were known to take care of the world tree Yggdrasil, which held the other nine realms of Norse mythology. Their care for Yggdrasil slowed down its death, as Norse mythology was centered on one belief that every living thing would die, and all existence would cease at Ragnarok.

Huginn and Muninn

Huginn translates to "thought," and Muninn translates to "mind." They were both ravens flying around and above Midgard, telling Odin of everything the men in Midgard were doing. Odin could monitor his tactics as the ravens moved to and fro, making him wiser about what was happening. These two creatures have often been connected to a metaphor for Odin casting out his thoughts and mind. However, the king of the Aesir gods was afraid that Huginn and Muninn might one day go and never return.

Trolls

In Norse mythology, there are various types of trolls. The first was the trolls that lived in the mountains and forest, which were very large, scary, and grotesque. The others were small trolls, like gnomes, that dwelled in deep caverns and underground caves. These specific types of trolls were described as not too intelligent but full of evil. The small gnome-like trolls could show kindness in exchange for favors, regardless of their nature. It was believed that the creatures were rocks, detaching and forming into the boulders seen all over Scandinavia. Some of these rocks were used as weapons by the trolls, while other rocks were trolls turned to stone by the sun. Valkyries

Anyone being wined and dined at the great Aesir king Odin's Hall must have had some connection with these creatures, the Valkyries. The Valkyries were female spirits that rendered services to transport the souls of dead and dying warriors to Valhalla, the heavenly home of the king of Aesir gods, where they awaited Ragnarok. Valkyries were noble and elegant. The name Valkyries means 'choosers of the slain.' However, despite their relationship with Odin's heaven, they did not solely serve the king of the gods but also decided who was loved or killed in battles, using their malicious magic to choose the souls they wanted.

CHAPTER NINE
THE PRESENCE OF KINGS AND PRIESTS IN NORSE PAGANISM

The literature of Norse mythology is linked to various legends concerning human heroes and kings, which added to the supernatural creatures' concentration within divine realms. There are different stories about Norse founders of clans and kingdoms, and these stories are crucial to explaining their national origins and proper history. As a result, Norse mythology may have had a closer relationship with tribal identity. There is no doubt about the physical existence of many Norse mythology characters, which has led many Scandinavian scholars to try to separate history from myth within the sagas.

Kings

In ancient Norse mythology, the title of king was incomplete and less supreme than could be seen in other history books and cultures. Norse hierarchy included three classes of people. There were those strictly bought and sold as enslaved people called the Thrall, then there were the middle-class farmers and peasants called the Karland, and finally, there was the class of aristocrats called Earls. The Earls were usually the only warlords with a reputation for success. They were called the drott. These drotts were selected by their fellow warriors who felt they had leadership qualities and were fit to be their leaders. The warriors paid homage to them. While at war, they acted as the leaders, and during peaceful times they also served as chieftains.

It is from the class of Earls that a petty king or chieftain was chosen. By default, these kings only had jurisdiction over a portion of land and its people. It was a position of honor bestowed on war successors based on merit or for being old and wise. The people in the community would usually make him king or chief of them all and pay homage and allegiance to him. They would give him gifts and allow him to make decisions over political and even religious events concerning the people.

However, that position was not one of great power. All kings were subject to regicide if they became too powerful or tried to be overlords. Instead, the position was more honorary and limited. In ancient Norse paganism, this chieftain or king held the job of providing the sacrifices demanded by the priest or priestesses for various rituals. He also had duties within the rituals and was a direct link between the priest and the people.

A hall was usually established in ancient Norse days. In these halls, endowments, religious events, marriages, and political discussions were held between the king and his people, or, at least, those who paid allegiance to him. By default, this king would also have to be a follower of the community deity and show allegiance by offering regular sacrifices for his people and the land over which he reigned.

Since the position of a king was mostly ceremonial and not inherited, their authority was also limited to a section of the realm and nothing more. Several kings whose roles were notable enough to have been recorded in Norse mythology. Although there is little to prove the truth or the story of these kings, they were the most notable throughout the long-surviving years of the Norse tradition.

They included;

Ragnar Lothbrok, Ivar the Boneless, Rollo of Normandy, Erik the Red, Leif Erikson, Freydis Eriksdottir, Hastein, Harald Fairhair, Harold Bluetooth, Sweyn Forkbeard, Cnut the Great, and Harald Hardrada, who was the last of the Norse kings.

Priests

Different professions existed in Norse paganism and culture. However, they never took on the character of professional or semihereditary druidical Celtic classes. However, a few reasons may have been responsible for this. Women were responsible for maintaining the aspects of shamanism tradition. However, there were also Völvas in Norse mythology, meaning the male ritual professionals were not fully recognized and were restricted from certain activities. In Norse mythology, certain people only held ritual activities, and the usual beliefs within the Germanic society and tradition of kingship sprang from the office of the priesthood.

The role of the priests was consistent with the same role god played. A kindred group of family's heads was responsible for the administration of sacrifices. Norse paganism had pagan priests who were referred to as hofgothi. These priests were the Norse gods' ministers. Hofgothi referred to an individual responsible for taking care of the gods' temples. While a hofgothi took care of the temple, a gothi was an individual leading religious ceremony. Usually, this would be a king, earl, or chief. This can be confirmed in the sacrifices made at Uppsala, where King Horid was the leader of the sacrifices, with the local priests assisting him.

Priests in the Norse religion usually shaved their heads using scores of rituals, painting some of their body parts black such as the upper ears, lips, and even eyes. Historically, there is no proof that Norse paganism had what could be recognized as professional priests. However, members of the communities were responsible for carrying out religious events, conducting other social functions, and holding other positions. In the society of Old Norse, religious authority was attached to those who were not overtly religious. In the Icelandic Middle Ages, godi, as stated earlier, was a social role that combined political, judicial, and religious activities. The Uppsala sacrifices occurred once in a blue moon every nine years (another use of the number 9 concerning the nine worlds) for individuals who had, on average, lived for three decades. That period between ceremonies was not short.

Up to a point, a visit to Uppsala could be likened to the pilgrimages to Rome before the introduction of transportation. However, there were differences in how Norse pagans practiced the Norse religion. This may have resulted in those in Uppsala following different practices and rituals than Danish, Icelandic, or Norwegian Norse pagans. Unlike some pagan practices, Norse pagans didn't have oracles or priests dressed in frightening costumes with no eyes. Their priests dressed the same as the Norse pagans and had the same relationship with the Norse gods as the pagans did. They could also read the signs much better than other Norse pagans. As far as we can possibly know, there didn't appear to be any need to provide the Norse gods with offerings or too much attention. The Norse pagans would take part in certain services at certain times of the year, like harvest or when asking for favors from the gods. Also, in Viking times, the Norse pagan priests first appeared to give sacrifices and perform religious ceremonies. The Uppsala high priest questioned Athelstan, asking him to deny the Christian god three times. Suspecting and discovering what Athelstan was carrying (a crucifix), he considered what to do. However, the priest was knowledgeable enough about the Christian religion to understand their imagery or symbols, of which most Norse pagans had no idea. Then the priest would offer the blood of different animals to the gods as a sacrifice. The animals would then be hung around the temple in the sacred grove. A priest would be given the responsibility of preparing the psychedelic mushrooms for Rollo, and Jarl Borg and priests in Yol would lead the winter sacrificial celebrations.

CHAPTER TEN
ANCIENT SYMBOLS AND DEPICTIONS

For as long as we can remember, symbols and depictions have been part of human civilization, even before the introduction of writing and speaking. Evidence has been found of the earliest pictures and signs made by humans, and these have been found everywhere, including on the walls of ancient caves. Some of the most frequent designs used in ancient places were handprints, lines, and dots. While these drawings help in pre-history, they also help their discoverers remember how events unfolded in the past or what they were similar to. However, there have been frequent suggestions that these symbols were also helpful in communication among people. Moreover, pictorial signs and symbols may also have been the earliest ways of expressing ideas.

On this note, the Old Norse pagans were not left out among other ancient religions that used symbols and depictions, especially among their gods and goddesses. The pagans attributed many ancient symbols and depictions to their deities in Norse mythology. Norse paganism has always been fascinating to people, both then and now. Thanks to their ancient symbols and depictions, many people in today's world are familiar with some Norse gods and goddesses. While many have some of these signs and depictions hanging on the wall, others use them as necklaces. Norse ancient symbols and depictions play an important role in our culture.

Norsemen in Norse mythology had different representations of their identity, religion, and faith which used symbols. One of the things believed about symbols is that they are magically powerful and can create a connection between the people, the deities, and the spiritual world. At some point, they were so powerful that Norse pagans believed these symbols could be used for powerful spells. Norse pagans derived lots of importance from symbols due to the powers they held for protection. Norsemen were fierce and brave seafaring warriors. However, they needed everything to survive in unfriendly weather conditions and terrains and engage their enemies. Despite their fierceness, they had to rely on divine protection to ensure that they would be freed from their enemies' attacks. As a result, many Norsemen used sigils to chase or ward off enemies as they believed sigils had this power. Norse paganism included the use of certain symbols and depictions, and the most popular ones among them were:

Runes and its Significance

The Old Norse mythology was based on Norsemen and different religious practices and speaking in Old Norse. This Old Norse was the language of the North Germanic people who spoke in three distinct dialects. These included Old West Norse, Old East Norse, and Old Gutnish. Old Norse was one of these dialects that eventually led to some of the Icelandic and Scandinavian languages used today. The Icelandic language used today is believed by many to be the closest to Old Norse.

However, what was the relationship between the Norsemen's mythology symbols and the depictions found on Runes?

In the same way that many countries have their own alphabet, the runes were the alphabet used in some Germanic and the Old Norse language during and before the Middle Ages. At the time, all Norsemen used the runic script to write Old Norse. Norsemen popularly referred to the runic alphabet as Futhark, based on the first six runes' names. While the Old Norse wasn't outdated, the Futhark had existed for a longer period. Therefore, the Futhark was made of three major generations. Among these three major generations of Futhark was the oldest generation or Elder Futhark. This specific generation was in use until the eighth century and comprised 24 runes. The oldest runes have been dated back to the second century AD. However, there are chances that the Norsemen used them even before this era.

The next one among the runes was the Anglo-Saxon Futhorc. These specific runes were used between the fifth and eleventh centuries, with 26 to 33 runes. The Younger Futhark was the last among these runes, having only 16 runes and the Norsemen used it between the ninth and eleventh centuries. The Norsemen used these runes to write during the era of the Vikings. When the era ended, the Latin script came as a replacement for the runic script. Naturally, runes used phonetics. A sound was derived from each letter and depended on the sound produced by each letter. Each rune had a name and a meaning, which became a symbol that represented something - an emotion, object, or, more commonly, a phenomenon. Different meanings may have been associated with the rune. Moreover, interpretations of runes may also have varied based on the direction in which they fell.

As an example, when some runes are read in reverse, they represent the direct opposite meaning of the run read the right way. The Elder Futhark contains 24 runes, and these are the best-known ones today. The runes fall into three separate categories and eight groups, with each set called an aett (plural aettir.) It is worth knowing that these runes are named after the Norse mythology characters. There are two major gods and goddesses in Norse mythology as discussed earlier. They include the Aesir and the Vanir. However, these deities have runes connected to them and what they represent in Norse mythology. Here are the 24 runes of the Norse mythology.

Fehu and its Significance

The first of the Elder Futhark runes is Fehu, depicting cattle or wealth and most associated with surplus, wealth, control, success, and hope. On the other hand, the meaning of Fehu may be far from what would normally be expected when read in reverse. Read in reverse, it could mean the loss of property or valuables that a person has worked hard to achieve. This sigil was often used by the Norsemen to bring luck and wealth. The Norsemen used this sigil for bringing back wealth and luck.

Uruz

Of all the Norse mythology runes, this refers to oxen or bull, associated with physical and mental strength, energy, speed, endurance, and hard work. It was also connected with potential, independence, and masculinity. It all centered on using strength to overcome difficult times and become successful. When the runes are read in reverse, they show impulsivity, chaos, sickness, frailty, and ignorance. The Uruz rune was typically used when an individual was required to gain strength to carry out a task or to continue with a task they had already started.

Thurisaz

This rune represents a thorn or giant and is associated with conflict, violence, and external forces, ungoverned by anyone or anything, that strongly influence someone's life. It was all about safeguarding oneself against those distractions which prevent you from moving forward. This was just like how plants are shielded from a predator by the presence of a thorn. Norsemen, as a result, used this rune as a protective symbol. Read in reverse, Thurisaz depicts a lack of defense, pitfalls ahead, and betrayal.

Ansuz

This rune was a symbol of the gods and indicated that divine messages be revered. Ansuz was sometimes known as Odin's rune, representing the Aesir king's wisdom. Odin was often called "the AllFather, a supreme being among the gods in Norse mythology. The rune was associated with advice, love, truth, insight, organization, wisdom, and wellness. It also had a connection with the exchange of information and communication. It symbolizes delusion, manipulation, and a lack of communication when read in reverse.

Raidho

Raidho was associated with transit and was sometimes referred to as a chariot or wagon. It is connected to transit on the spiritual level or the physical world. The rune also had associations with evolution, a change of place or scenery, rest, and negotiation. Depending on the circumstances, it could also mean a need to make a decision. In reverse, Raidho would mean evil, rigidity, and dislocation in some way. The Norsemen often used this rune when they needed to travel and required protection.

Kenaz

In Norse mythology, Kenez was a symbol of light, typically a torch or lantern, representing creativity, faithfulness, inspiration, wisdom, and a clear, enlightened path ahead. It appears to indicate a previously unseen light, perhaps an indication that the way ahead had previously been obscured. Read in reverse, Kuraz indicates stagnation and darkness and a feeling of confusion and being lost.

Gebo

Gebo indicated gifts that may have been physical but also an exchange of something between two people. An individual became the giver, and the other became the receiver. Gebo was also a depiction of love, partnership, and relationships. When you read Gebo in the reverse direction, the meaning remained the same.

Wunjo

Wunjo is a rune that refers to joy. Therefore, it depicts special attention, wealth, celebration, security, triumphant sense, and success. The light that comes from a happy person is called Wunjo. When you read Wunjo in a reverse direction, it is far from expected as it depicts unhappiness, loss, feeling lost, or strange.

Heimdall's Aett

Heimdallr was the ruler of these sets of runes. In Norse mythology, Heimdall was the powerful god guarding Asgard among other Aesir gods. Asgard was the Aesir god's abode. Heimdall usually stayed on top of the Bifrost (the rainbow bridge that served as a link between Asgard and the human world) to observe anyone likely to invade, and he used his hearing and sight power. With his powers, Heimdall could hear and see all that went on between the worlds. In Heimdall's aett, the runes were associated with the energies and external forces required to create, grow, expand, or anything else that could about change.

Hagalaz

This is the first rune in Heimdall's aett and is associated with the destructive forces of nature - the name Hagalaz translates to "hail." It is impossible to control these forces as they occur as uninformed, indicating changes that cannot be avoided or prevented in an individual's life. However, the impact of these inevitable changes depends on an individual and the steps taken toward it. The amazing thing about this rune is that it doesn't have any negative meaning or depiction when read in a reverse direction, making it one of the few runes with no negative meaning when reversed.

Naudhiz

Naudhiz symbolizes needs. It meant a need that depicts survival, the ability to triumph over difficulties, and the need for change. The rune Naudhiz is connected to self-perseverance and reflection. Naudhiz is used when an individual's needs require evaluation, when their needs and wants need to be differentiated. In reverse, it is associated with depression, starvation, and distress.

Isa

Isa means ice and is associated with stagnation in spiritual and physical terms. It is also associated with clarity, calm, rest, and becoming stuck in a rut. The rune symbolizes frustration and difficulty. Isa has no contrast meaning when you reverse the position.

Jera

Jera also appeared in Heimdall's aett and was representative of the wheel of the year or the harvest. It was an indication that something had to have been worked on. Jera was also a symbol of surplus, sufficiency, wealth, prosperity, lifecycle, energy, and transformation. When you read Jera in reverse form, the meaning remains the same.

Eihwaz

Eihwaz symbolized a yew tree and represented longevity and a regenerative ability. It was also known that the yew tree's seeds were poisonous. The tree was also known to consist of poisonous seeds. Eihwaz depicts security, changes, death, power, and defense. The reversed reading can signify annihilation, weakness, and disorganization.

Perthro

There are uncertainties surrounding Heimdall's aett alphabetical rune as its specific meaning is still not clear. However, its shape suggests that Perthro may be a dice cup and indicates that fate has intervened in a person's life and that the individual should make the best they can from what's happened. Perthor also had associations with rebirth, magic, secrets, and fate. Being related to mysteries, its reverse direction depicted faith loss, seclusion, and immobility.

Algiz

The Heimdall aett rune, Algiz, is also known as the elk or protection rune. It is a symbol of protection against evil or danger and is associated with defense, connection to the divine, and guardianship. Algiz showed harm that was yet to be presented, warnings, and a disconnection from the divine when it is read in reverse.

Sowilo

Sowilo meant sun, and it was connected to the power to change things positively, energy, good health, luck, victory, and happiness. Sowilo had no negative meaning when you read it in reverse form.

Tyr's Aett

Tyr's aett is the next set of runes. Tyr was the god of war, the sky, and justice, and his rune offered Norsemen significant meaning. The runes in this aett are linked with divine deities who were trying to teach humanity what it needed to know. It was also believed that the wisdom and knowledge humans gained from the gods gave them some control over cosmic energies and allowed them to transform into divine beings.

Tiwaz

The first rune in Tyr's aett is Tiwaz, a derivation of the name Tyr and it was the symbol of a warrior. It is associated with boldness, governance, victory, strength, self-sacrifice, and order. Read in reverse, it indicates unrest, chaos, imbalance, apathy, and blocked creativity.

Berkana

The Berkana rune is a symbol of mental and physical growth. It symbolized a new start, fertility, reproduction, regeneration, and healing. Read in revere, the rune indicates a takeover, infertility, problems in the household, rigidity, and a lack of control.

Ehwaz

The Ehwaz rune symbolized a rune movement or horse and was associated with physically moving, forging ahead, transit, and continuity. It was greatly connected to transformation, relationship, energy, and encouragement. Reading Ehwaz in reverse form symbolized transformation, need, unrest, carelessness, and confinement.

Mannaz

Mannaz was a rune in Tyr's aett that referred to man, representing the self, including the communication between individuals. Moreover, Mannaz signified social structure, knowledge, and craftiness. The reversed reading of Mannaz depicted dissociation, being short of help from others, and manipulation.

Laguz

Laguz was significant to water or lakes, symbolizing how an individual feels emotionally. It was also a symbol of flexibility, mysteries, immediate apprehension, loss of the mind, and the hidden. It depicts shortened creativity, craziness, freight, and obsession.

Ingwaz

The Ingwaz rune was named for Freyr, a Norse mythology god who was also known as Yngi. He belonged to the Vanir and was the god of prosperity, the human world of Earth, and fertility. Ingwaz depicts wellness, harmony, growth, family affection, masculinity, and peace. The meaning of Ingwaz remains unchanged when you read it in reverse form.

Dagaz

Tyr's aett rune Dagaz referred to day or dawn. It was connected to change, fresh starts, accomplishment, breakthrough, awakening, and information. Like a few other runes that retain their meanings when reversed, Dagaz also falls into this category.

Othala

The Othala rune is connected to the ancestors' properties and symbolizes lineage, inheritance, possessions, heritage, and the home. Othala was connected to the family, and, read in reverse, it could be associated with wretchedness, misfortune, and prejudice.

Runic Inscriptions

According to Norse mythology, the Norsemen used staves and twigs to write the runes. The staves were straight lines, while the twigs were diagonal lines coming off the staves. Because they were linear in nature, they could be carved into many objects, an important factor in the Viking Age, given that paper and ink were unavailable. Some of the runes with engravings were made from metal, wood and bones. However, most of the runes are no longer in existence due to the Norsemen preferring wood above all else to write on. Among the existing runes, writing has been found on metal and stone, and some of the common objects include weapons, coins, and other things people would use in their daily life. Most objects are inscribed with the owner's name or the person who engraved them. Runic inscriptions have also been found on large stones, and these were typically done in honor of the tribe leaders and the dead. Some inscriptions tell stories of Viking voyages, and, these days, many of these rune stones can still be found all over Scandinavia. Norsemen were not used to a good writing culture when comparing Norse Paganism to other religions. There was an oral transfer of their cultural beliefs, lifestyle, and stories. Up until the 13th-century, the sagas of the Norsemen were never put into documentation form. Some poems and sagas were written in Iceland and certain countries during this period.

Gungnir

Norse mythology tells us that Gungnir was Odin's trusted, magical spear. It was forged for him by the Nidavellir dwarves from one of Yggdrasill's branches. The spear is imbued with many magical properties, one of which was that it never missed its target and would always return to Odin once its mission was complete. We can trace Gungnir's accuracy in the rune carvings, and when Odin journeyed to acquire the ultimate in wisdom, he used Gungnir to sacrifice one of his own eyes.

Odin used Gungnir to create fear among his enemies. Gungnir was responsible for intimidating them to the point that they felt threatened. One popular belief about Gungnir is that if an individual died by this weapon, such an individual would transit to Valhalla after his death. Gungnir, in connection with Odin, held massive power and strength according to the belief of the Norsemen. Therefore, they fabricated their weapons to look exactly like the mythical Gungnir. They also went to the extent of carving runes on these weapons.

The Norsemen attested to the fact that this mythical weapon required significant strength, skill, power, concentration, accuracy, and great authority. According to legend, Gungnir's power was so strong that when an oath or wish was made before the spear, it would come true. Another belief strongly associated with Gungnir is that whenever Odin threw the spear, it would fly across the sky, leaving a flash of bright light that looked like a shooting star. The old saying, "wish upon a shooting star," can be traced back to this.

Mjolnir

Mjolnir was unarguably the most popular symbol among the many other Norse mythology symbols. Its popularity also rose after being referenced in the Marvel comics and movies. Known as the symbol of hammer god Thor, Mjolnir remains one of the most powerful weapons. Although its look has not been the same over the years, Norsemen greatly respected it. Mjolnir was often depicted as looking like a short sledgehammer, which meant the hammer could easily be wielded with one hand. It is commonly believed that the dwarves forged the hammer in Svartelheim, the same dwarves who crafted Gungnir.

According to the mythology, Odin, king of the Aesir, was Thor's father, the Norse god of lightning, thunder, and the sky. Thor was Asgard and Midgard's protector, using Mjolnir's power to wage war against the dark forces and giants. Being the lord of the sky, Thor was also in charge of agriculture, encouraging fertility and growth. Should there be no air or water, the agricultural crops could not survive. Thor was associated with fertility and growth, and it was believed that Thor used Mjolnir to consecrate marriage, births, and deaths. Many amulets have been found from the Viking Age containing a Mjolnir symbol. The symbols also appeared on runestones and tombstones during the era.

The Norsemen held a high reverence to Thor and gave great significance to the symbol Mjolnir during the time of the Vikings. During important ceremonies, Norsemen would invoke Thor to bless and protect them. For example, during a marriage, Norsemen believed that when lightning and thunder were produced during the ceremony, the marriage would be fertile and healthy, and the union would be consecrated.

Norsemen also believed that lightning and thunder were produced when Thor battled and defeated the giants. Mjolnir was said to symbolize protection and power, keeping Midgard safe, preventing trouble, and bringing about complete harmony.

The Triple Horn of Odin

The triple horn of Odin also went by the name of the Horn Triskelion and was a Norse mythology symbol commonly used by the Norsemen. The symbol depicts a trio of interlocked horns and the story of Odin's journey to get the Poetry Mead. At some point, the Aesir and Vanir were against one another, according to Norse mythology. As a result, the dispute escalated into conflict between the two sects of gods. At some point, they were tired and had had enough. Therefore, they called a truce, which ended the conflict between them. To bring the war to an end, both sects came together and chewed some berries and spat them into a container. However, their spit led to the emergence of a man known as Kvasir.

It was believed that Kvasir was wise enough to answer whatever questions were asked of him. He was always on the move and visited many different realms, passing on his wisdom to each one. On his journey, he stopped at the dwarf realm, Svartalheim, where he met a pair of dwarves named Galar and Fjalar. The dwarves sensed the magical properties in Kvasir's blood, and both pretended they wanted to talk to him in private. The dwarves slew Kvasir, took his blood, and mixed it with honey, resulting in the Poetry Mead. Myth tells us that if a person drank the mead, they would become a scholar or poet.

Sleep thorn

"Sleep thorn" is a rough translation of the Norse mythology symbol. It symbolizes sleep, rest, and health. When the Norsemen were not traveling or in battle, they lived agrarian lives. It was said they did all they could to live healthy lives, with plenty of sleep to refresh them for each new day. Sleep thorn were carved on bedposts in every Scandinavian home. The symbols were also found in Norse text throughout the Viking Age, but there seems to be a certain amount of variation in where the Sleep thorn symbol originated. Today, Sleepthorn is depicted as a row of four harpoons, and, in terms of applying it, the symbol is described as a physical object meant for throwing at the enemy. In other cases, its description is that of a spell that can be cast wherever or toward whatever seems applicable. Norsemen believed that this symbol was used in causing one's adversary to fall asleep deeply, especially when on the battlefront. It was hard to wake them once they had gone to sleep. Sleepthorn was considered so effective that enemies could not awaken until whoever applied the Sleepthorn wanted them to. When all enemies are deeply asleep, one could enjoy the advantage of easily defeating them. However, it also had various functions according to different sources.

Valknut

Norse mythology tells us that the Valknut was often known as "Odin's knot" and was seen as a sacred symbol. It was associated with death and was a symbol of the cycle of life, the journey we all make from birth to death. The symbol shows a trio of interlocked triangles, indicating a connection between the divine and Odin. Valknut had nine corners, one for each realm or world.

The name, Valknut comes from two words. First, Valr, translated as "slain warrior," and second, Knut, translated as "knot." According to Norse mythology, some of the warriors who died in battle would be taken by the Valkyries to Valhalla. The Valkyrie were female warriors considered powerful and who were responsible for determining the fate of a dead warrior. They could allow a warrior entrance to Valhalla to join other slain warriors but also has the power to refuse them.

Those dead warriors who did gain entrance to Valhalla would remain there until Ragnarok, when they would join Odin in the final battle. The Valkyrie would choose which warriors they wanted in Valhalla, transporting them there by wolf or winged horse. Valhalla was Odin's great hall in heaven, and the chosen warriors would eat and drink what they wanted as they waited for Ragnarok. It was also one of the five realms after death in Norse mythology.

As a result, Valknut depicts the life cycle, the point where an individual journeys from life to death and the transition from one realm to another. Many Norsemen had the Valknut symbol carved on their tombstones. Valknut was said to have provided protection to the slain warriors on their journey to Valhalla.

Valknut was associated with Odin and was shown in many pieces of artwork depicting Odin. One example is the Stor Hammars stones from Sweden in the 7th century, depicted in a popular image.

The Matrix of Fate

The Matrix of Fate was also called Skuld's Net or the Web of Wyrd and is one of Norse Mythology's most common symbols. The Norsemen used this symbol to depict the interrelationship between the past, present, and later dates. Norns in Norse mythology weaved the symbol Web of Wyrd or Skuld's Net. The nornsz, a group of three maidens, represented what had passed, what was happening, and what was to come. Norns were responsible for determining a human's fate in the world. They also referred to them as destiny shapers. When the Norns wore the Matrix of Fate, it gave them the ability to determine the fate or destiny of a given individual. The Matrix featured nine staves, all intersecting to give the appearance of a net. A rune would be depicted in the spaces between the staves when the Norns wanted to see a given individual's past, present, and future. According to the Norsemen, fate was determined at the birth of a child. They also believed that every human would pass through the events of fate, including the gods, as there was no discrimination with destiny. For instance, the gods had a fate, which was believed to be Ragnarok. While there are no records to prove that Skuld's Net was used in the Viking Age, there is a belief that the Matrix of Fate was extensively used in the Norse way of life.

Helm of Awe

In much the same way as Aegishjalmur, the Helm of Awe was seen as a magical protection sigil. It was also seen as a symbol of boldness and strength. There were eight lines on the Helm, each coming from the center, looking like tridents forming a circle. A closer look at the symbol appears to show the trident defending the center. The Helm of Awe was painted on many Norsemen's foreheads when they went to battle as they believed it would help protect them. Norsemen believed that Aegishjalmur was so powerful that it could cause enemies to become scared in a fight, even to the extent that enemies who set eyes on the Norsemen's foreheads were faced with defeat.

The symbol of Aegishjalmur was found in the Galdrabok, the Icelandic spellbook or grimoire from the 17th century. This appears to suggest that the symbol had magical properties and was used in casting spells. It is commonly suggested that the magical properties come from how the Helm of Awe was made, and a closer look at it reveals that a pattern is formed on the sigil, made by several runes. For example, the center circle is formed from the Elhaz rune. Because the Helm was seen as magical, it was depicted on certain items to ensure a protective spell could be successfully cast. As such, the symbol was painted or engraved on different objects, including tree bark, drinking horns, soil, and even the Norsemen's own bodies.

The Helm of Awe was also mentioned in the Poetic Edda, a collection of Norse poems recorded in 13th century Iceland. Fafnir, a mythical dragon, was talked of in one poem called Fafnismal. According to the myth, the dragon was the first to possess the Helm and claimed that his magical powers could be traced back to it. Sigurd was a Norse hero responsible for eventually killing the dragon and taking Aegishjalmur into his possession.

Vegvisir

Norsemen referred to Vegvisir as their Wayfinder or compass whenever they seemed lost or wanted to trace a certain direction in Norse mythology. The usual belief about this symbol was that it had the power to guide Norsemen to their headed destination. For instance, when Norsemen were out at sea, the chances of the weather changing were reasonably high. They may have witnessed rainfall or stormy weather that could have been dangerous at sea during those times. Whenever this happened, the Norsemen found it very difficult to navigate the ships due to imbalance and visibility, which could result in getting lost at sea.

Norsemen prevented these situations by using Vegvisir as a compass to help them locate where they were headed, and at times, they used it to guide themselves to safety. However, it remains unclear how the Norsemen wielded this symbol when facing danger or loss of direction. In Norse mythology, Norse pagans believed that the Vegvisir guided and protected the crew from dangers at sea whenever they found themselves in such situations. Vegvisir was, therefore, used as a ship's talisman.

While the Norsemen applied the powers of the Vegvisir mostly at sea, its powers went beyond sea applications. Onshore Norsemen believed that the Vegvisir was very powerful. Hence, many of them applied it when they seemed to have lost their way in the spiritual realms. The vegvisir has been seen many times over the centuries, in many different places. The first vegvisir symbol was found in the 19th-century Huld manuscript. Like the Helm of Awe, it had eight staves forming a circle, each stave representing a cardinal or intercardinal point. At the end of each stave was a motif made of curves, dots, and small lines. The Norse pagans believed that Vegvisir should not be regarded as a symbol of the Vikings because a significant time may have passed before its documentation. Therefore, the available evidence is not enough to confirm that the Vikings used Vegvisir in their era. The illustrations on the Viking ships used runes and played a pivotal part in the mythology. It was suggested that the symbol is and always has been valid in Norse mythology.

Swastika

The swastika was a popular symbol in Norse mythology and symbolized spirituality in various cultures in different parts of the world. The German NAZI party used the swastika as a symbol of representation in the 1900s. After this happened, different people worldwide have come up with many controversies about the symbol swastika. This symbol was greatly used in Norse mythology to depict life force, fortune, sanctity, and power. There is also said to be a connection between the sun wheel, the swastika, and Mjolnir. Like Mjolnir, the symbol adopted by the German party was also used in the consecration of objects and people. The Norsemen believed that the swastika was a symbol of safety and luck, frequently carving it into tools and other objects to ensure they were sacred. The Norsemen believed that their work would be more productive when they used tools with a swastika carved on them.

Overall, though, the Norsemen's preferred symbol was a combination of Mjolnir and the swastika, both Thor's symbols. It is thought that the Mjolnir amulet worn by Norsemen may also have had a swastika carved on it. Norsemen also believed that the swastika had so much power it could be used to make a spell more effective. It was believed to add power to the spell, making it more potent, and is one of the reasons why so many runic inscriptions have been found with the symbol on them. Runic inscriptions were also believed to contain powers that could also be used as magical spells. To round it up with this symbol, many people carved this symbol on the tombstones of their loved ones. This was done to wish them good luck and an effortless journey to the life hereafter.

Yggdrasil

Yggdrasil's images have surfaced in different cultures' mythology. It symbolized the link between everything and life's cyclical nature. Death is not the end of everything. All things have an eternal state – and natural – transformation. The world tree Yggdrasil has been regarded as one of the most powerful symbols and depictions of Norse mythology. Yggdrasil is believed to be the bridge that connects the gods' world and men's world. The nine worlds existing, both physical and spiritual realms, were rooted in the roots of Yggdrasil and the realm of the giants Jotunheim, the location of Mimir's Well of Wisdom.

However, there is much left to discuss on this issue as the general belief was that the world tree was an ash tree with its name interpreted as "Odin's Horse." This was the tree to which the Allfather tied his horse, while Yggdrasil could also mean the "tree of terror." The All-father hanged himself on this same Yggdrasil as a sacrifice in his quest for wisdom. In the root of the world tree, Yggdrasil, is located the death-dragon Níðhöggr gnawing at the roots, while the discord eagle has its nest in the upper branches of the world tree. Ratatoskr, a squirrel, moves to and fro on the trunk of Yggdrasil, conveying messages between the dragon and the eagle. Níðhöggr, eagle, and Ratatoskr symbolize change as the world tree will not last until eternity. In Ragnarok's final battle, the gods' twilight and the world's end, the world tree will be destroyed along with everything else. However, the new world will give room to the rebirth of Yggdrasil again.

Huginn and Muninn

Being mysterious creatures in Norse mythology, Huginn and Muninn symbolized certain things in Norse mythology. Odin's ravens were said to stand for memory and thought and, in the same way as vultures, they saw a battle's aftermath as a feast. Muninn and Huginn were symbols of Odin and Valhalla, where heroes went after they died. They also symbolized transformation and death. There is typically considered to be a connection between birds and gods, and this can be seen in depictions of Odin and his ravens.

Birds were used as ceremonial sacrifices in the Viking Age and were also used at funerals and other ceremonies. This was considered a part of the victory at Uppsala. However, ravens were the birds of delight to offer as a sacrifice. They were also a symbol of life and helped Odin in his journey. We often see Muninn and Huginn depicted on cremation urns and other death-related objects. The ravens symbolized Odin's intellectual aspects but would signify memories and thoughts of the deceased to ordinary mortals.

CHAPTER ELEVEN
NORSE MAGIC

Whenever we hear the word magic, we understand different things, but the most common understanding is that it involves incantations or enchantments with the spirit world. We may also believe it includes casting spells or charms to communicate with the supernatural world. Whatever you may think magic is about, the truth about magic and Norse paganism is that they are related. However, the Norsemen also communicated with the spirit world, as seen in their different religious practices. An example of this is shamanism, where a Shaman is believed to have been to the spirit world and returned possessing the power to cure all ills.

The Norsemen engaged in different practices of magical arts. They were regarded as professionals and were accorded respect for their professionalism, and their respective community valued their services. According to Norse literature, both men and women were engaged in the practice of magic by wielding magical arts. It was also stated in other places in Norse literature that when men were involved in these magical arts, they were up against women who were so powerful, the men risked damage to their reputation and manhood. Although women mainly carried out Norse magic, sagas mentioned that men and women engaged in these practices.

Lots of magical and cult practices took place in the Norse religion, and the most important magical practices took place in the domain of housewives. In this situation, the woman of the house would play the role of priestess or gydja. The Northern people considered women to be holy humans who have had massive magical powers even from the time of the old Germanic tribes. They also considered women to hold specific power to talk about the future, especially what it holds, a reverence that lasted in Scandinavia until the introduction of Christianity. As a result, Norse magic greatly involved women in general, especially women who took part in the arts of magic and paganism.

Generally, Christian accounts, especially those that described how the Norsemen converted, hold a hostile view of Norse paganism and the practices of magical arts. Some of these views include the demotion of gods to devils, criticisms of Norsemen as evil sorcerers, and more. As a result, Norsemen who took part in a pagan context were considered practitioners of the worst evil deeds. The further removed the account during the era of paganism, the more inaccurate and confusing the accounts become. This confusion is demonstrated in the concepts of seiðr and spá.

Women's magical art and religious activities had the usual connections with social acceptance and their defined roles. At times, their magical practices and religious activities reflected the responsibilities of their home. Other times, magical arts and religious practices were in contrast to the expected social roles of women. This acted as an outlet for anger or frustration, but they hated men who defined the responsibilities of a woman in her environment. The same goes with magical practices and art in the era of the Norse women. A Norse woman during the era of the

Norsemen discovered magic in her spindle. She intertwined the spells into her family clothing's thread, revenging herself using powerful sorcery skills.

In what is referred to as "magic" today, Norse magic, also called seidr, was a common act in Norse mythology. Both Norsemen and Norse women (major women, known as völva) who took part in magical practices occupied socially enigmatic roles. As a result, they were feared by many. Moreover, people accorded them more respect and, at the same time, people could look down on them. Amid crisis and unsettlement, societies largely depended on them by drawing from their well of knowledge.

They turned their magical practices, which have always been executed indoors, into public cult displays. However, some magical practices connected to seiðr are spá (which involves telling or forecasting fortune), omen or signs interpretation, shapeshifting, and galðr.

Galdr is a form of magical practice (usually a song) that involves unleashing magical powers and granting access to other realities. The Aesir king Odin was also known as the father of galdr (galdrs faðir). In Falsetto, a galdr was sung. A man that wanted to perform the magical art of galdr was required to put on women's clothing. Additionally, such a man was required to imitate a woman's voice. However, each galdr does not have the same effect. Galdr are of different types, and each has a varying effect. For instance, Norse women or Norsemen who tried to raise the dead had a specific galdr to sing, and this was different from the galdr they would sing for an individual seeking to ease their worries. There were also different galdr to heal sick people, remove poisonous substances, weapon blunting, fire prevention or stoppage, safety from distress, fooling witches, the power to be invincible, chain breaking, and lots more.

The secret wisdom was embedded in another galdr. Another magical practice in Norse religion was shapeshifting. This was mainly a part of the ritual in shamanism. It was widely believed that people who practiced this type of magic held the power of separating the body and the soul from each other. When they separated the body from the soul, they could transfer the soul into an animal, traveling to different parts of the world. It is worth noting that the practices of seidr were not only uncommon but also, many did not like it. A man could be accused of ergi if he were to practice seidr. Ergi had a partial translation of "being unmanly," which could result in being an outcast. The Norse trickster god Loki in the Lokasenna was seen to lay into the Æsir king Odin, accusing him of having engaged in the practice of seidr.

The old Germanic people saw magic as a normal way of life. People involved in the practice worked with certain principles that were believed to be below the cosmological workings instead of opposing them. Imagine that an individual who engages in magical practice is separated from the rest of his people. In this case, the individual's level of knowledge generally related to the cosmos and the center of the working world. Magic vocabulary used in Norse mythology was based on the concept of knowledge, and a Norse magic specialist called Professor Catharina Raudvere said that "kunna, a verb, refers to "to know," "to understand," and "Knowing by heart." It also refers to having deeper knowledge and insight of ancient traditions and folklore. To that end, magic has a general common word which is

"fjölkyngi." However, the word is derived from kunna, translated as 'massive knowledge."

Furthermore, and the idea of techniques in magical practices and knowledge of the beings that took part in them, fate was seen as another form of knowledge. This magical art was prevalent among the Germanic people. The Norsemen understood the importance of destiny. However, it did not mean they held a fatalistic view of it. Instead, understanding it should focus on knowing what the future holds to ensure it remains under some kind of control. Norsemen also engaged in divination rituals. This magical practice was based on expressing the ways to access the hidden parts of reality and quantifying what was given. The divination's outcome marked an individual's free will and limits, and after this, there could be a way to act within these limits. As a result, the Norsemen held great views about forecasting, interpretation of dreams, and even curses. Hence, they treated them with utmost attention and care.

They were responsible for showing the tension between being free and depending on others. Nevertheless, the terms may seem confusing. The belief in destiny could be defined as an individual's freedom. And there are set limits lying within the human condition for their identification and acting within the scope given. Also, other important themes in sagas are people's decisions or choices and their consequences in the long run. Everyone has a fate or destiny. However, different chances lie ahead for everyone to develop varying strategies for connecting with major structural time perception. When the Norsemen practiced magic, they were said to have focused on fate or destiny and helping an individual achieve their purpose. Today, when we talk of magic and its many practices, we are talking about two types and the distinction between them "white magic" and "black magic." They believe that white magic is all about kindness and being good, while the latter is primarily based on doing or committing evil. This is a common belief among people across the world. However, the pre-Christian Germanics never had these conceptions of magic, and they also didn't have any real views of it. Although little is known about them, indigenous categories were said to exist in Germanic practices. Old Norse magic was not tolerated by Germanic people. Known as seidr, these practices were thought to be female-only ritual magical practices. Men who engaged in it were termed unmanly, like the Aesir god-king Odin. Men who took part in magic typically went into having no specific complex of "warrior shamanism" in which initiatory military communities took part. Galdr is an old word in Norse mythology that comes from the word galán to crow. This indicates magical practices were based on enchantment or runes and may be referred to as another specifically arranged magic system. However, there are many uncertainties, just as there is insufficient evidence.

The most common practitioners of seidr during the Norse period were the Norns. They were used to weaving to establish all human destiny or fate, an indirect reference to seidr techniques, given the duties of magic, they applied those techniques. As a result of this relationship, anyone who took part in magical practices was often referred to as a norn (Old Norse for "witch") with a lowercase "n." The two categories (Aesir and Vanir) of the Norse gods and deities were also practitioners of magic, especially the All-father and Freyr. Both deities were typical examples of deities engaged in magical arts, representing both genders. As mentioned before, in Norse mythology, magic was seen as gendered. Freya was the archetype of the volva and was a professional goddess who was active in magical art. She was also considered responsible for introducing the Norse gods to seidr.

The volva carried out their magical acts, moving from place to place as they did so. A Völva engaged in this to get a room, board, and other pleasing gifts. The saga of Erik the red has a very detailed account of a woman who engaged in such practices. However, other sagas mentioned it as well, including some heroic poems. (This is notable in Völuspá, "The Insight of the Völva"). It contained different references to people who engaged in seidr activities. The Völva was distinguished from her wider society negatively and positively, just like other Shamans. People sought after her massively, and she was widely praised and exalted, feared, and in some cases, reviled.

Völva is a replica of veleda, (a prophetess people accorded massive respect among the people of Germania for many years). Over centuries, veleda, a respected and molded goddess, turned into Freyja, and both roles involved magical practices. The woman held a more respected role among the people even when there were variations in dignity over time.

CHAPTER TWELVE

MYSTICISM AND ANIMISM IN NORSE MYTHOLOGY

Different people use various definitions of the word mysticism. The truth about this is that the Norsemen also engaged in it. It is sometimes referred to as becoming at one with the gods and may also refer to attaining the insight of truths unknown to humans, which different experiences and practices support. These practices may include spiritual beliefs, especially when it has a connection with the occult. Norse mythology had many gods, and the most supreme among them was Odin. As the supreme patron among other Norse gods, he was a mystic personality or element of Norse worship. As a result, Norsemen and Norse pagans of today's world regard him as a role model for seeking knowledge from beyond, including mystics and forecasting.

Odin, the All-father, had many achievements, ranging from creating the Earth (Midgard) in which humans lived to create the human species. However, none of these accomplishments seems to have been difficult for him. He was also believed to have engaged Ymir in a fight and labored on Midgard's creation. Despite this, the All-father does not seem to have offered anything as a sacrifice to achieve this. However, in his quest to become more knowledgeable than any human could have thought, the All-father made some incredible sacrifices on two different occasions. One of these occasions was when he plucked out his eyes at the well of Mimir, lying there dead for nine days. However, there is a lesson the All-father passed on from this occasion; to have a deeper knowledge of the world's architecture and the path of fate comes at great cost, and even for the gods, there is a price to pay. However, it could be the most valuable thing to achieve beyond any other material thing.

Animism in Norse Mythology

Animism refers to the practices and knowledge of taking part and obeying gods and spirits living in different objects, including landscapes. Norsemen, during their time, believed everything in existence had a specific purpose and a place. They believed that nothing existed on its own and that every object had a certain spirit that occupied them, including a deity or a god. This is why Norse religion was polytheistic, animistic, and pantheistic. According to the belief system of Norse mythology, every object, both animate and inanimate, possessed a soul. They believed that weather, rivers, rocks, plants, animals, and other objects had a distinct spiritual essence. This can be seen in Shamanism, where shamans had to invoke the spirits before they were allowed to fetch certain items like leaves.

Chapter 11: Present-day Practice of Norse Paganism

Norse mythology existed over a thousand years ago with different gods, religious beliefs, ritual practices, and sacrifices to appease the gods. Different gods also existed, and the Norsemen revered these gods by performing blót (in the Old Norse religion). However, the introduction of Christianity seems to have put an end to Norse paganism. Today, many people worldwide still worship the Norse mythology gods, and it doesn't appear that Norse paganism will soon go into extinction. Even in the 21st century, there has been continued interest in the Norse beliefs. Most people are informed that the Norsemen practiced the Norse religion. Moreover, many people are familiar with some of the most popular Norse mythology gods, such as Odin and Thor, especially as several movies have been released about the gods, keeping them forever in our minds.

In spite of this, one question is still commonly asked about Norse religion - "Is it still in existence, and is it still practiced?" Even today, the different Norse pagan religions, including Asatru, have different followers, all committed to Norse god worship. Asatru is one of the most established forms of the religion, still practiced today, but many people still refer to it as "Odinism" or "Heathenism." Despite different terms used in expressing the ancient Old Norse religion, the truth about it is that there are not too many differences in their beliefs across the world.

Many may have also read, or are familiar with, the beliefs of the Norsemen system of old Scandinavia, where the Norsemen embraced and practiced the Norse religion. It may even not be difficult for some to name some of the most popular gods of Norse mythology, such as Odin, Thor, and Loki. How is the practice of Norse paganism in the present-day world different from how the Norsemen worshipped their gods in the Viking era?

Amazingly, some of the Norse mythology gods are still going strong after a thousand years, even after the Viking era. Many people believed that the introduction of Christianity brought a total end to the Nordic religion and the belief in the Norse gods. On the contrary, the Norse religion is still going strong, welcoming massive followings from time to time. Norse pagans still continued to practice the religion secretly after Christianity arrived, some even practicing under the cloak of the new religion. Today's world has seen adherents of the religion of the Norsemen, between 500 and 1000 in Denmark. These people still believe in Norse mythology, worshipping its ancient gods from time to time.

The Modern-Day Norse Paganism Practice

During the era of the Norse men, they were used to gathering in the open air. However, the modern-day Norse pagans did not deviate from the same practice method as the Nordic believers also met in the open air. When the modern-day Nordic believers gather, they appear to their gods by praising them and offering them. They pay their respects to the gods, drinking toasts in their honor and partaking in feasts. However, the toast may not be made to all gods at the same time. For example, Norse pagans may only want to honor Nj ǫ rðr, the god of fertility. In this case, their toast is made only to Nj ǫ rðr. However, if they want to be more prosperous and want their harvest to be a good one, they make their toast to Frej instead. Modern Norse believers can also make their own personal toasts. For example, a young woman who wants to fall pregnant or wants to find their one true love can make a toast to Freyja. Women facing challenges or other problems would need to worship Thor and ask for his help in providing them the strength they need. For Nordic worshipers who are short of wisdom, the All-father Odin will grant their request when they praise him according to their beliefs. Modern-day Norse pagans' belief in their deities and gods is not a direct continuation of what the Norsemen believed during their time. Today, Nordic religion followers base their worship on reviving the old beliefs and reinterpreting them in their own way since there are few surviving written accounts. However, some short accounts of Nordic religious practice were written by Christian monks, typically in the form of sagas. Despite the number of new religions worldwide, even after introducing the popular Christian religion, Norse paganism continues to win the souls of many, even without evangelizing them. According to the statistics from Iceland, there was a rise in the number of adherents belonging to the Norse religion. There were about 1,040 followers of the Norse religion about a decade ago. Amazingly as of the 1st of January 2017, the number had jumped to 3,583 followers of the Norse religion. Since 2007, there has been a rise of about 244%. The figure shows that the Norse religion has been the fastest-growing Icelandic religion over the past ten years.

This figure shows that the Norse religion has leapfrogged other religions by 1% of the Icelandic population for the first time in a thousand years.

What Does Asatru Mean?

Asatru (also referred to as Asatro) refers to the worship of Norse mythology gods. Asatru isn't just about worshipping the Norse gods; followers also worship the ancestors and giants. One thinning you should know is that the term "Asatru" or "Asatro" is relatively modern, not becoming well-known or used much until the 19th century. When Christianity arrived, Norsemen didn't give it a specific name. Instead, they called their religion "the old way" or "Forn Sidr," in direct contrast to the new religion of Christianity. The biggest Nordic society is found in Denmark, also called Forn Sidr. With more than 500 followers, the Dutch Forn Sidr was established in 1997, and in 2003, it was given society approval, becoming the only official approved Nordic society. Moreover, Nordic adherents in Denmark organize themselves in groups in different locations in Denmark. While Nordic believers choose to worship in groups, some choose to be alone in worship. Adherents of the Norse religion are also present in some countries such as Iceland, Norway, and Sweden. Great Britain and the United States are also some countries with a few groups of Nordic believers.

The Revival of an "Old Way"

The Norsemen's' beliefs were reinvigorated by believers in Old Nordic, using myths handed down orally and recorded in different documentations. The main sources of these myths are the Younger Edda and the Elder Edda. However, because no real interpretation of these sources exists, the Norse religion was practiced in a way that each Nordic believer got their own meaning from it. To benefit from the power of the Old Norse gods, today's believers visit pre-Christian age cult sites and carry out offerings and sacrifices to the gods. Where they go varies, as some followers choose to visit the site of a ship burial while others may go to a Bronze Age burial mound. A "Gydge" is a female cult priest, while a "Gide" is a male cult priest, and they lead the Norse believers who do the sacrificial activity. The usual practice is that these members form a ceremonial circle, giving them the chance to create "a holy space." The holy space refers to the portal to the Norse gods and deities' realm, with the Norse worshippers paying obeisance to their gods until a ceremonial opening of the circle one more time. Norse pagans invoke the gods relating to the specific season and the sacrificial theme that goes with it. They will make their offerings at up to four different times during the year, including the winter and summer solstices and the spring and autumn equinoxes. The winter solstice celebration is on the shortest day, and the summer solstice celebration is on the longest day, while the two equinoxes have a day and night of equal length. The following are some things you should know about modern Norse paganism or Asatru.

How the Norsemen divided the year was greatly connected to their daily work and life activities, using the course of the sun and the moon's phases. The Norsemens' yearly calendar began on or around October 13th. When the winter half of the year began, it was marked and celebrated with a public offering of sacrifices and the harvest. The end of this period was marked with a victory sacrifice correspondent to how the period started. This would be held on or around April 14th, when spring officially started and the new war season began.

These days, the winter solstice is celebrated on December 21st, roughly halfway between the start and end of the period and the shortest day of the year. Once the day passes, the following days gradually get lighter and longer, with the sun slowly beginning to strengthen its warmth. One of the biggest festivals celebrated in this half of the year is Christmas. Norsemen would use the summer half of the year to gather their supplies to see them through winter. On June 21st, the longest day of the year, the summer solstice was and still is, celebrated as Midsummer's Eve. When the celebrations were over, the days began to shorten and get darker, and, at the autumn equinox, the night and day lengths were equal. The darkness ate up the light once more, and the winter half would begin again.

NOTE

www.ingramcontent.com/pod-product-compliance
Lightning Source LLC
LaVergne TN
LVHW071649300125
802570LV00009B/265